SCOUT TESTS
AND HOW TO PASS THEM

CENTENARY EDITION

SCOUT TESTS

AND HOW TO PASS THEM

CENTENARY EDITION

MICHAEL O'MARA BOOKS

First published in Great Britain in 2013 by
Michael O'Mara Books Limited
9 Lion Yard
Tremadoc Road
London SW4 7NQ

A CIP catalogue record for this book is available from the British Library.

Papers used by Michael O'Mara Books Limited are natural, recyclable products made from wood grown in sustainable forests. The manufacturing processes conform to the environmental regulations of the country of origin.

ISBN: 978-1-78243–143-5 in hardback print format
ISBN: 978-1-78243-170-1 in ebook format

1 2 3 4 5 6 7 8 9 10

Editors: Louise Dixon, George Maudsley, Katherine Parker
The Scout Association: Chris James
Designed and typeset: Ron Callow, Design 23
Illustrations: The Scout Association.
Additional illustrations: Pages 36, 121, 184, 256 Clipart.com;
148, 279 Dennis Barbulat/Shutterstock.com

Printed and bound by CPI Group (UK) Ltd, Croydon, CR0 4YY

www.mombooks.com

CONTENTS

Foreword by Bear Grylls   11

Tenderfoot Tests   13

Badges

Ambulance   *25*

Artist   *36*

Athlete   *37*

Bee Farmer   *42*

Bird Warden   *47*

Blacksmith   *50*

Boatman   *53*

Bugler   *62*

Camper   *66*

Carpenter   *72*

Clerk   *74*

Coast Watchman   *82*

Cook   *88*

Cyclist   *98*

Electrician   *101*

Engineer   *108*

Entertainer   *109*

Farmer   *110*

Fireman 114

Friend to Animals 116

Gardener 121

Handyman 122

Healthy Man 131

Horseman 142

Interpreter 148

Laundryman 149

Leather Worker 152

Mason 153

Master-at-Arms 156

Metalworker 173

Miner 174

Missioner 177

Musician 184

Naturalist 185

Oarsman 186

Pathfinder 188

Photographer 190

Pilot 195

Pioneer 213

Piper 221

Plumber 223

Poultry Farmer 226

Printer 232

Prospector   *235*

Public Health Man   *240*

Sea Fisherman   *244*

Signaller   *245*

Stalker   *256*

Starman   *257*

Surveyor   *269*

Swimmer   *270*

Tailor   *274*

Telegraphist   *279*

Woodman   *280*

Approved Publication, issued under agreement with the Boy Scouts' Association, London.

FIRST STEPS

1 D. Net. **1 D. Net.**

IN

SCOUTING

COMPLETE INSTRUCTION IN TENDERFOOT AND SECOND CLASS TESTS

JAMES BROWN & SON,
Official Scout Publishers, GLASGOW.

Please Note:

This is an edited version of the 1914 original text of *Scout Tests*, which ran to almost 700 pages. The huge array of badges found in the original book is breathtaking in itself, but the detail within each badge was extraordinary. This edition gives the reader a 'taster' of each badge, and an authentic flavour of what it was to be a Scout 100 years ago. Readers should remember that the content of this book has been drawn from historical sources and does not represent current good practice or advice. The Scout Association and the publisher disclaim any liability for any injury, accidents or loss that may occur as a result of information or instructions given in this book.

Approved Publication, issued under agreement with
the Boy Scouts' Association, London.

FIRST CLASS TESTS

1D. Net.   **1D. Net.**

AND HOW TO PASS THEM

JAMES BROWN & SON,
Official Scout Publishers, - - GLASGOW.

FOREWORD

by Bear Grylls, Chief Scout

Scouting has always had its badges – but why are they still so popular? One reason is that Scouts love to show their achievements: from camping, climbing and emergency aid to cooking, circus skills and even street sports, Scouts still wear their badges with great pride. Badges promote self-sufficiency and resourcefulness; they inspire Scouts to continue learning, to teach others and develop new skills.

This book from a century ago shows just how much has changed; although we still have a badge that tests a young person's cooking skills, the Cook Badge from 1914 shows how to prepare a savoury goose for six people – with all the trimmings – as well as a dish called Bowline Hash. It's nothing if not ambitious. Just the names of the badges are evocative in themselves, from Bee Farmer, Poultry Farmer to Plumber and even the Miner Badge, these were serious and demanding tests. The Sea Fisherman demanded experience of catching fish at sea using trawls, nets and lines – no mean feat for a twelve-year-old! The Boatman badge, meanwhile, encourages young people to familiarise themselves with the names of the 47 sails of a tall ship.

The badges were highly practical, even vocational and were designed to prepare young people for the world of work. Some of the language and terminology is unfamiliar today – as part of the Printer Badge, Scouts were encouraged to set up a handbill and familiarise themselves with paper types such as the Royal Quarto. But the basic principles are all recognisable, it is packed with sensible advise and many of these old badges could feasibly still be tackled.

So this book is in part a history lesson and partly a reminder that Scouts from 100 years ago were not so different from those of today. They wanted adventure, the opportunity to try new things and the chance to prove themselves.

Enjoy these tests – and if you like what you read, perhaps you would consider joining the great Scouting adventure that continues to this day.

BEAR GRYLLS
CHIEF SCOUT

TENDERFOOT TESTS

It should be noted that a tenderfoot may not wear the buttonhole badge until he has passed the Tenderfoot Tests. The tests are as follows:

Test No. 1

Know the Scout Law.

The Scout Law

1. A Scout's Honour is to be Trusted. If a Scout says, "On my honour it is so", that means that it is so, just as if he had taken a most solemn oath. If a Scout were to break his honour by telling a lie, or by not carrying out an order exactly when trusted on his honour to do so, he may be directed to hand over his Scout badge and never to wear it again. He may also be directed to cease to be a Scout.

2. A Scout is Loyal to the King, and to his officers, and to his parents, his country and his employers. He must stick to them through thick and thin against anyone who is their enemy or who even talks badly of them.

3. A Scout's Duty is to be Useful and to Help Others. And he is to do his duty before anything else, even though he gives up his own pleasure, or comfort, or safety to do it. When in difficulty to know which of two things to do, he must ask himself, "Which is my duty?" – that is, "Which is best for other people?" – and do that one. He must Be Prepared at any time to save life, or to help injured persons. And he must try his best to do a good turn to somebody every day.

4. A Scout is a Friend to All, and a Brother to Every Other Scout, no Matter to What Social Class the Other Belongs. Thus, if a Scout meets another Scout, even though a stranger to him, he must speak to him, and help him in any way that he can. A Scout must never be a SNOB. A snob is one who looks down upon another because he is pooer, or who is poor and resents another because he is rich. A Scout accepts the other man as he finds him, and makes the best of him.

5. A Scout is Courteous. That is, he is polite to all. And he must not take any reward for being helpful or courteous.

6. A Scout is a Friend to Animals. He should save them as far as possible from pain, and should not kill any animal unnecessarily, even if it is only a fly – for it is one of God's creatures. Killing an animal for food is allowable.

7. A Scout Obeys the Orders of his parents, patrol leader or Scoutmaster without question. Even if he gets an order he does not like, he must do as soldiers and sailors do; he must carry it out all the same because it is his duty. That is discipline.

8. A Scout Smiles and Whistles under all difficulties. When he gets an order, he should obey it cheerily and readily, not in a slow, hang-dog sort of way. Scouts never grouse at hardships, nor whine at each other, nor swear when put out. When you miss a train, or someone treads on your favourite corn – not that a Scout ought to have such things as corns – or under any annoying circumstances, you should force yourself to smile at once, and then whistle a tune, and you will be all right.

9. A Scout is Thrifty. That is, he saves every penny he can, and puts it in the bank, so that he may have money to keep himself when out of work; or that he may have money to give away to others when they need it.

10. A Scout is Pure in Thought, Word and Deed. That is, he looks down upon a silly youth who talks dirt, and he does not let himself give way to temptation, either to talk it, or to think, or to do anything dirty. A Scout is pure and clean-minded and manly.

Scout Signs

Scout signs on the ground or wall etc., close to the right-hand side of the road:

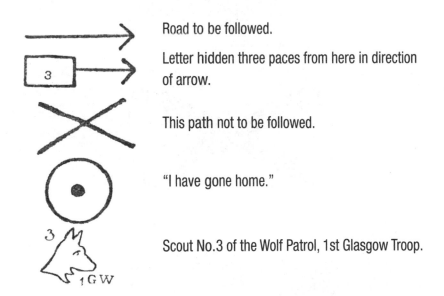

Road to be followed.

Letter hidden three paces from here in direction of arrow.

This path not to be followed.

"I have gone home."

Scout No.3 of the Wolf Patrol, 1st Glasgow Troop.

At night, sticks with a wisp of grass round them, or stones, should be laid on the road in similar forms, so that they can be felt with the hand.

Test No. 2

Know the composition of the Union Jack and the right way to fly it.

The Union Jack is the national flag of the United Kingdom and the British Empire, and is made up of the old national flag.

British Union Flag. In 1801 a red diagonal cross with a white border, representing the white flag with a red cross of St.George

Patrick of Ireland, was added to the flag, making the Union Jack of Great Britain and Ireland as we know it today.

Test No. 3

Tie the following knots: reef knot, sheet bend, clove hitch, bowline, fisherman's and sheepshank. The tenderfoot should also be shown the practical use of the knots. For instance, it is not sufficient merely to be able to tie the "bowline". The tenderfoot should be shown how to tie the loop round himself and round another Scout.

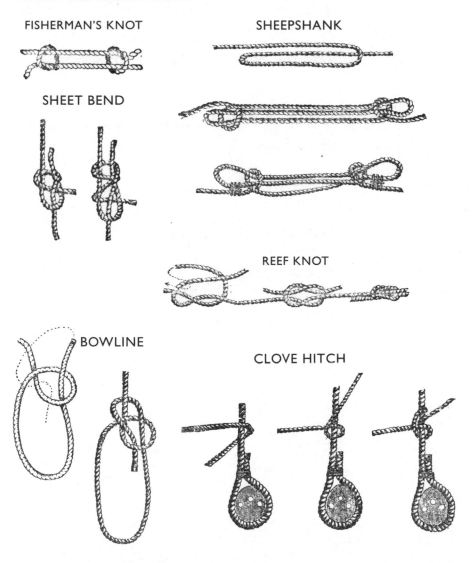

FISHERMAN'S KNOT

SHEEPSHANK

SHEET BEND

REEF KNOT

BOWLINE

CLOVE HITCH

The Scout's Promise

The Scout's Oath is as follows:

> "I promise on my honour that I will do my best
> 1) To do my duty to God and the King.
> 2) To help other people at all times.
> 3) To obey the Scout Law."

The Scout Law

It is perhaps rather difficult to remember the different heads of the law. The following is easily learned and is a good way of memorizing the headings:

> ' *Trusty, loyal and helpful,*
>
> *Brotherly, courteous, kind,*
>
> *Obedient, smiling and thrifty,*
>
> *Pure as the rustling wind.*"

SECOND-CLASS TESTS

Test 1

Have at least one month's service as a tenderfoot. That is to say, one month from the date of having passed the Tenderfoot Tests and taken the oath, not from date of joining.

Test 2

Elementary first aid and bandaging – see chapter on the Ambulance Badge.

Test 3

Know the Semaphore or Morse sign for every letter in the alphabet. To qualify for this test it is not sufficient merely to know the alphabet. The Scout should be able to send and read any letter given, and a few short easy words.

Test 4

Track half a mile in twenty-five minutes; or, if in a town, describe satisfactorily the contents of one shop window out of four, observed for one minute each; or Kim's game, to remember sixteen out of twenty-four well-assorted small articles after one minute's observation.

Test 5

Go a mile in twelve minutes at "Scout's pace". It should be noted that the mile has to be done in twelve minutes, not in less than twelve minutes. The object is to practise the test so that it is done as nearly as possible in exactly twelve minutes.

Test 6

Lay and light a wood fire, using not more than two matches. The mistake usually made by a tenderfoot is to start with too large a fire. Sufficient wood should first be collected and kept at hand.

Test 7

Cook a quarter of a pound of meat and two potatoes without using cooking utensils other than the regulation billy. This, of course, should be done on the fire made for Test 6.

It would seem superfluous to say that this test should be done in the open air, and not in the home, but the writer has heard of cases where this test has been done indoors.

Test 8

Have at least sixpence in the savings bank.

Test 9

Know the sixteen principal parts of the compass.

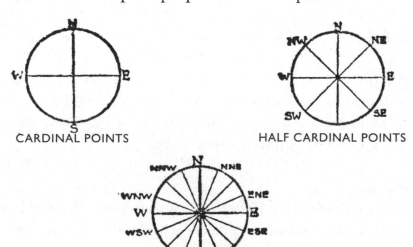

CARDINAL POINTS   HALF CARDINAL POINTS

INTERMEDIATE OR
THREE LETTER POINTS

FIRST-CLASS TESTS

Test 1
Swim fifty yards. (This may be omitted when the doctor certifies that bathing is dangerous to the Scout's health.)

Swimming The art of swimming is not difficult of attainment and it is an art which every boy should acquire. The first thing a Scout has to overcome is "water-funk". Everyone who cannot swim is more or less a water-funk, so that the beginner must not think himself peculiar in that respect. Given confidence, your body will float. Having gained confidence in the water, the beginner can start learning to swim.

Test 2
Must have one shilling in the savings bank.

Test 3
Send and receive a message either in Semaphore, twenty letters a minute, or Morse, at the rate of sixteen letters per minute.

Test 4
Go on foot, or row a boat alone, or with another Scout, to a point seven miles away, and return again, or, if conveyed by any vehicle (railways not allowed) or animal, go to a distance of fifteen miles and back, and write a short report on it. It is preferable that he should take two days over it.

Test 5

Describe or show the proper means of saving life in case of two of the following accidents: fire, drowning, runaway carriage, sewer gas, ice-breaking, electric shock; or bandage an injured patient, or revive an apparently drowned person. The chief point in all these tests is that the Scout should "keep his head", and act promptly.

Test 6

Cook satisfactorily two of the following dishes, as may be directed: porridge, bacon, hunter's stew; or skin and cook a rabbit, or pluck and cook a bird. Also, make a "damper" of half a pound of flour, or a "twist" baked on a thick stick. This test must, of course, be done in the open air, over a camp fire or camp kitchen.

Test 7

Read a map correctly, and draw an intelligible rough sketch map. Point out a compass direction without the aid of a compass.

In drawing a rough sketch map, what is wanted is clearness, and nothing should be put in that is unnecessary for the full understanding of the sketch.

Test 8

Use an axe for felling or trimming light timber, or, as an alternative, produce an article of carpentry or joinery, or metal work, made by himself, satisfactorily. Before felling a tree, Scouts must be very careful to first get permission to do so, and to see that only trees that are pointed out for their use are touched.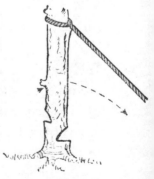

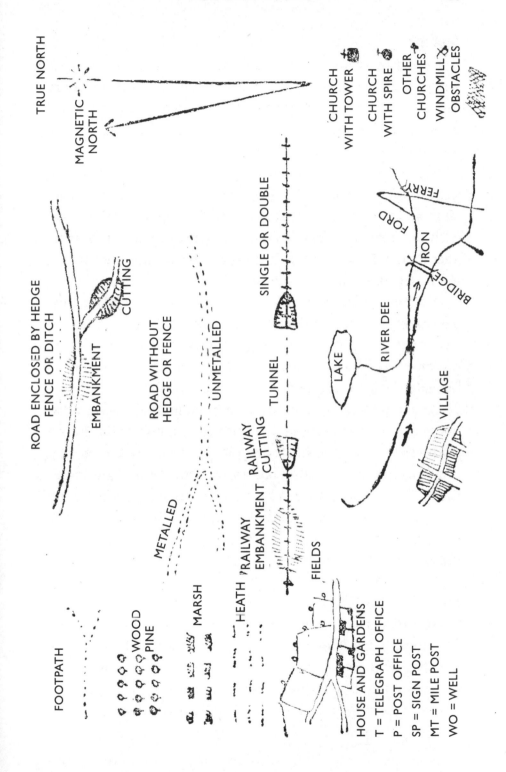

TRUE NORTH

MAGNETIC NORTH

CHURCH WITH TOWER

CHURCH WITH SPIRE

OTHER CHURCHES

WINDMILL

OBSTACLES

ROAD ENCLOSED BY HEDGE FENCE OR DITCH

EMBANKMENT

CUTTING

ROAD WITHOUT HEDGE OR FENCE

UNMETALLED

METALLED

SINGLE OR DOUBLE

TUNNEL

RAILWAY CUTTING

RAILWAY EMBANKMENT

FIELDS

HEATH

MARSH

WOOD

PINE

FOOTPATH

FERRY

FORD

IRON BRIDGE

RIVER DEE

LAKE

VILLAGE

HOUSE AND GARDENS

T = TELEGRAPH OFFICE

P = POST OFFICE

SP = SIGN POST

MT = MILE POST

WO = WELL

Test 9

Judge distance, area, size, numbers, or height and weight, within a 25 per cent error. Scouts should not be passed on one day's results. Two or three different tests should be given under varying weather conditions. The following points should be very carefully studied.

When training Scouts to judge distance, long distances should not be attempted at first. Each Scout should know to an inch what is his usual pace both walking and running. Ask each to name an object, say, 20 yards away, then ask him to pace it to see how far out he is. Increase the distances gradually up to 100 yards, say, 10 yards at a time.

A Scout should be able to tell accurately any distance by pacing. In the same way, if a cyclist, he should know the exact circumference of his front wheel, so that by tying a piece of rag round a portion of the tyre, and counting the revolutions, he will be able to calculate the distance covered.

Distance can also be fairly accurately judged by noticing how much time elapses between the flash from a gun or the steam from a railway whistle, and the report or whistle. Sound travels, roughly, 1,100 yards in three seconds. Therefore, by counting at the rate of 11 beats in three seconds (this can be easily acquired with a little practice), each beat will represent 100 yards. That is to say, if twelve is counted, at this speed, between the flash and the report, the distance would be 1,200 yards.

Test 10

Bring a tenderfoot trained by himself in the points required for a tenderfoot. It should be noted for this test that it is not merely sufficient to introduce a tenderfoot, but the Scout must also train him in the tenderfoot tests.

AMBULANCE BADGE

A Scout must know:

The Fireman's Lift.

How to drag an insensible man with ropes.

How to improvise a stretcher.

How to fling a life-line.

The position of main arteries.

How to stop bleeding from vein, artery, internal or external.

How to improvise splints and to diagnose and bind a fractured limb.

How to deal with choking, burning, poison, grit in eye, sprains and bruises, as the examiners may require.

*Generally, the laws of health and sanitation as given in *Scouting for Boys*, including dangers of smoking, want of ventilation, and lack of cleanliness.

Special Note: In this chapter, it is not intended to deal exhaustively with the subject of "First Aid".

We shall take the points in the order they are laid down for the test.

The Fireman's Lift

Turn the person face downwards and take hold of him close under the armpits. Raise the body as high as possible, bringing the arms down round the waist. Drop on the knees, take hold of one of the wrists and at the same time pass the other arm between the legs. The patient will then rest across the shoulders. The hand that is passed through the legs now grips the patient's hand as shown in the diagram.

THE FIREMAN'S LIFT

How to drag an insensible man with ropes

Tie a bowline round the patient's waist, bring the rope over the patient's head and tie another bowline there. Turn your back to the patient and tie a bowline round your own neck. Crawl out on all fours.

How to improvise stretchers

Stretchers are easily improvised with Scout poles. Turn the sleeves of two coats inside out, pass two poles through the sleeves; button the coats over them. Roll up another jacket to use as a pillow.

A door, gate or shutter, well covered with straw or sacking, also makes a serviceable stretcher.

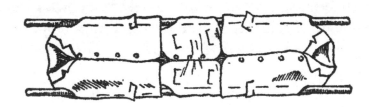

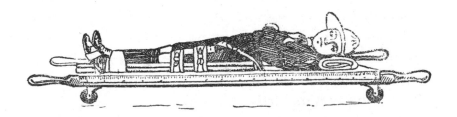

How to fling a lifeline

Practise throwing the line over a dummy, but first make sure that the end is fastened somewhere. The object is to throw the rope over the person to be rescued. If any object, such as a stone or cane, is fastened to the end of the line, care must be taken that it does not hit the person. If there is a current flowing, put a piece of wood or a life-buoy on the end, and throw it above the person, allowing it to float down to him.

How to stop bleeding from vein, artery, internal or external

For bleeding from the nose: place the patient in a chair, raise the arms above the head. Sponge the forehead and temples with cold water. Apply something cold to the top of the spine, such as a key, a penny, or the back of a watch. Plug the nostrils with cotton wool.

In all cases of bleeding, a Scout should nerve himself to overcome any feeling of faintness or sickness. Many people turn sick or faint at the sight of blood, but a Scout should say to himself, "I won't faint," and the feeling is quickly overcome. Remember: if you are alone with a friend who has seriously hurt himself, that his life may depend on your prompt action. If you give way to a tenderfoot's feelings, your friend might bleed to death.

After the bleeding has stopped, wash the wound with a piece of lint or cotton wool dipped in an antiseptic solution. Condy's fluid, which is a solution of permanganate of potash, is an antiseptic, and also a disinfectant, and is excellent for washing the wound. It is cheap and easy to make, two large tablespoonfuls to a pint of water being sufficient. Wash carefully but see that no blood clots are dissolved or washed off. The clots prevent further bleeding.

After washing, dress the wound with boracic lint. Boracic

lint should always be kept in a Scout's ambulance outfit. Failing boracic lint, use ordinary lint or cotton wool soaked in an antiseptic solution. When removing a dressing, don't try to pull it off, as this would restart the bleeding. Bathe it off with a piece of boracic lint, dipped in tepid water.

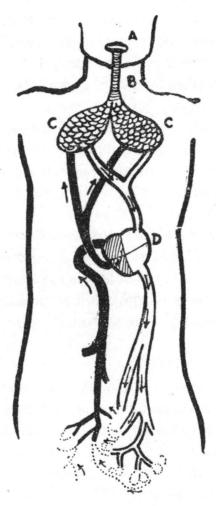

The arrows show the direction in which the blood flows.
A – Mouth.   B – Windpipe.   C – Lungs.   D – Heart.

Arteries.   Veins.   Capillaries.

How to improvise splints and to diagnose and bind a fractured limb

Diagnose, in this instance, means to distinguish between a fractured (that is broken) bone and a sprain or strain.

In the case of a fracture of a limb, the limb is shortened and the power of the limb lost; there is also unnatural movement where none should be. There is pain and swelling at the place of injury; but this is also present in the case of a severe sprain. Another sign of a fracture is "crepitus", that is to say, a grating sensation is felt when the broken ends of the bone are rubbed against each other.

Boy Scouts, however, should never try for crepitus, for, by doing so, they would almost certainly do further injury.

If not quite certain whether the bone is broken or not, no harm can be done by treating the limb for a fracture; that is to say, putting it in splints.

There are two kinds of fracture: simple and compound. The simple fracture is when the bone only is broken. Compound fracture is when in addition there is a flesh wound.

The first thing to do with a compound fracture is to stop the bleeding and dress the wound, then treat as for simple fracture.

With simple fracture, the object of first-aid treatment is to prevent further injury. To do this, it is essential to be very careful with the patient. Splints can be improvised by rolling a newspaper up tightly, or by using pieces of wood, a Scout staff, pieces of bark etc. A splint should be long enough to go beyond the joints both above and below the fracture. One splint should be put on each side of the limb. Something soft, such as folded bandages, cotton wool, neckerchiefs etc., should be placed between the splints and the limb.

Splints are fixed in position as shown in the following diagram

Triangular bandages are the only ones used in first aid. In place of a proper bandage, the Scout neckerchief folded diagonally will serve the purpose. If the neckerchief is used, however, great care must be exercised to see that it does not come in contact with the wound, because the dye from it might cause blood-poisoning.

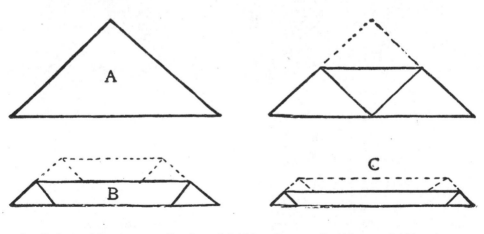

A – Full-sized bandage.   B – Broad fold bandage   C – Narrow fold bandage

ARM SLING   FOREARM FRACTURE

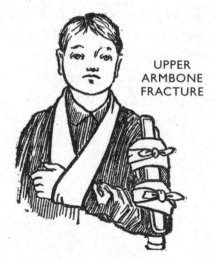

UPPER
ARMBONE
FRACTURE

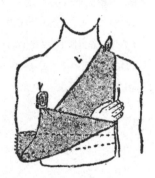

COLLAR-BONE FRACTURE

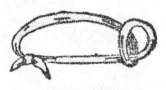

ALTERNATIVE
COLLAR-BONE FRACTURE

Choking: Loosen collar. Try to pull out the object with the forefinger, handle of a spoon, or other object. Two or three hard smacks on the back will sometimes dislodge the object. Send for the doctor.

For a bone in the throat, eat doughy bread. If small objects such as buttons have been swallowed, give a large dose of castor oil. If sharp objects such as needles or pins, do not give an aperient. Give crusty bread to eat.

If the substance is in the wind-pipe, send for doctor at once. Hold the patient upside down and he may choke it out.

Burning: Is fully dealt with under Fireman's Badge.

Poison: Always send for a doctor at once. Except in the case of the acid poisons, try to make the patient sick, by tickling the throat with a feather, or by giving him salt and water to drink, or mustard and warm water. Give him first some milk or raw eggs, which will collect the poison.

If the poison is an acid, when the mouth will be stained or burned, on no account should an emetic be given, as this would make him sick and burn the throat again as it came up. Give him white of egg, flour etc. (see List, overleaf).

For narcotic poisons, such as morphia, opium, etc., which make the patient drowsy, give an emetic, then strong tea or coffee; don't let him sleep; walk him up and down, slap and punch him to keep him awake.

Antidotes for Poisons: If possible, while awaiting the arrival of the doctor, give as follows, on List overleaf.

Grit in the eye: Don't rub the injured eye. Rub the other eye, and the tears may wash the object out. Roll back the upper

For

Bedbug Poison Blue Vitriol Corrosive Sublimate Lead Water Saltpetre	Give Milk, or White of Eggs, in large quantities
Sugar of Lead Sulphate of Zinc Red Precipitate Vermilion	Give Milk, or White of Eggs, in large quantities
Fowler's Solution White Precipitate Arsenic	Give prompt Emetic of Mustard and Salt – tablespoonful of each; follow with Sweet Oil, Butter or Milk
Antimonial Wine Tartar Emetic	Drink warm Water to encourage vomiting; if vomiting does not stop, give a grain of Opium in water
Oil Vitriol Aqua Fortis Bicarbonate Potassa Muriatic Acid Oxalic Acid	Magnesia or Soap, dissolved in water, every two minutes
Caustic Soda Caustic Potash Volatile Alkali	Drink freely of water with Vinegar or Lemon Juice in it
Carbolic Acid	Give Flour and Water or Glutinous drinks
Chloral Hydrate Chloroform	Pour cold water over the head and face, with artificial respiration, Galvanic Battery
Carbonate of Soda Copperas Cobalt	Prompt emetic; Soap or Mucilaginous drinks
Laudanum Morphine Opium	Strong Coffee, followed by ground Mustard or Grease in warm water to produce vomiting; keep in motion
Nitrate of Silver	Give common Salt in water
Strychine Tinct. Nux Vomic	Emetic of Mustard, aided by warm water

eyelid over a wooden match or pencil, and remove the foreign matter with the edge of a handkerchief, or a clean camelhair brush. A very good method is to dip a small, clean camelhair brush in castor oil. Shake off the superfluous oil, and apply under the lid.

Sprains: Apply cold fomentations and bandage the limb tightly. After a day or two, it is advisable to encourage slight movement of the joint, but still with the bandage on, otherwise the joint will become stiff.

Bruises and contusions: Apply cold fomentations at once, so as to prevent as much effusion of blood as possible.

WARNING: This advice is no longer current; always seek expert up-to-date first aid advice.

ARTIST BADGE

A Scout must draw subjects:
From memory, and state on each drawing when and where he
    saw the subject drawn.
From sight.
From imagination.

The three drawings pasted onto a single sheet of brown paper to be submitted to Imperial Headquarters, with certificates from Local Association that they are the original work of the candidate and that all three drawings have been completed in two hours (*not* two hours each).

ARTIST AT WORK

ATHLETE BADGE

A Scout must:

Demonstrate the proper method of sitting, standing, walking, running and starting a race.

Give proof of proper training and of taking regular bodily outdoor exercise.

Pass 1 running test, 1 jumping test, the throwing test and the Scout mile test.

To become proficient enough to obtain this badge requires good health, energy, willpower, grit, all-round physical ability, a clear understanding of the training necessary and a knowledge of the splendid effects of this training.

Perhaps some Scouts will be inclined to say, "Oh, I haven't got all these things, these qualities, so how can I get the badge?" Well, of course not, very few of us have at the start. Now, what is the first thing to do in starting out to win this badge? Yes, win is the right word, because one has to struggle and, whenever there is a win, it is always the result of a tussle. Well now, the first thing is to try. And there isn't a Scout living who is unable to try. Once this decision is taken, it is in itself the first step in the development of willpower. To make an actual start requires energy and to keep on requires grit, to keep on keeping on develops all-round physical ability, and when these things are practised with understanding, the result will not only be the proud possession of the Athlete's Badge, but that feeling, that condition, of health and strength, which contributes so much to success in life. Further, to feel big, healthy and strong makes one ever ready to help others, and thus the training for, and the gaining of, the Athlete's Badge is the becoming of a good and true Scout in every sense of the word.

Sitting: Many people think the correct sitting posture is uncomfortable; this is because they have the wrong idea of what the position should really be. It is thought the body must be held in a kind of stiff, erect, pokerlike attitude. Certainly, it must be erect, but not stiff and stilted. The seat is the first consideration. A large portion of the thighs should rest on the chair; that is, the bottom of the back should be within about two or three inches from the chair back, then the back will be held nearly vertical.

The head should be held easily erect, the neck being pressed back. This is the correct poise when sitting and it is beneficial and less tiring because it allows freedom of the breathing apparatus, the digestive organs and the free action of the nervous system. The drooping head, rounded back, and sagging stomach is a position giving undue pressure to heart, lungs and stomach and the healthy working of these organs and the free flow of energy is hindered, hence that tired feeling.

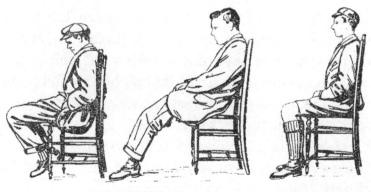

BAD POSITIONS   GOOD POSITION

GOOD POSITION   BAD POSITION

Standing: If the correct position of sitting has been thoroughly mastered, standing should present little difficulty. Generally speaking, the feet should be astride with the weight of the body equally balanced on both legs, the hands just hanging loosely by the sides. This, of course, is the easy correct standing posture. Having given attention to the instructions regarding the body for the sitting position, another correct position is to stand at attention, so that there are really two correct standing positions, which might be termed passive and active. The simplest instruction for the active position of attention is to stand up as straight as possible, mentally and physically on the alert: head erect, chest raised, shoulders slightly back, knees straight, feet open nearly at a right angle, elbows straight, fingers stretched. To make the position quite perfect, the body may be swayed slightly forward so that a little pressure with the toes has to be made to prevent the body falling forward. The body must be kept straight. This swaying movement really takes place at the ankle joints and thus the position to begin walking is arrived at.

Walking: The left or right foot is carried forward and a free swing of arms begun. In good walking it is necessary to realise that as the left foot is carried forward the right knee should be straightened, and vice versa. This point is the secret of good walking. The aim is to glide along with practically no bobbing up and down. If a Scout bobs up and down a lot he is using much energy to do this instead of using the energy to move forward.

Running: Running should be done on the toes with the arms bent. In fact, the arms may move in a similar manner to the horizontal piston on a railway engine. When doing long distances, start on the toes, breath through the nose and carry on running like this for a time. It is a mistake to think this can be done always and all the time. It is a little theory often found in books, which has no practical foundation.

Starting: Starting is a position of readiness to be off on a given signal. It is not merely a physical position, for the mental aspect is a very important factor. One foot must be placed on the mark and the other a little behind, with the body in a forward stooping position, fingers just touching the floor or the arms bent. Then the brain must be on the alert and this is where you get the coordination; that is, the working together of brain and muscle. If a Scout is fit and healthy, he will be off like a shot on the crack of the pistol. When on the mark, he must fix his eyes on the direction he means to travel, no looking around, no wavering. He listens, and on the signal being given, brain and muscles act, while he gets away almost like lightning. Concentration is the thing: look ahead – listen – move.

Running is a splendid thing for wind and limb. It has

been said that we breathe through our legs, meaning that whenever we move our legs quicker we breathe quicker and improve both wind and limb.

Diet: A Scout should know that plain food is best. Good white and brown bread and butter, fruit, vegetables, meat and puddings of various kinds should be regarded as proper nourishment. There is no need for a fanciful diet whether in or out training.

BEE FARMER BADGE

A Scout must have a practical knowledge of swarming, hiving, hives and general apiculture, including a knowledge of the use of artificial combs etc.

The best time of the year for a beginner to start bee-farming is in May. As a hobby it is a most interesting and healthy one; moreover, with care and attention, it can be made a paying one, and a nice little addition to a Scout's income can be made by attending to his bees during his spare time.

The first thing to do is to make or buy a hive. The old-fashioned "skep" covered with straw is being entirely replaced by the modern frame hive, which is just a wooden box filled with frames. The frames are four pieces of wood, nailed or joined together. The size of the standard frames on the market is top bar 17 inches long, bottom bar 14 inches long, and depth 8½ inches when hanging in the hive.

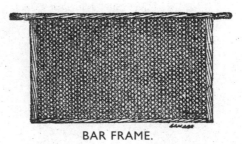

BAR FRAME.

FRAME HIVES.

Having got the hive ready and the frames filled with foundation, purchase a good swarm, one with a young queen. The queen should not be kept beyond the third year, and if the bees themselves do not depose their monarch, the bee-keeper should remove her and put another younger queen in her place.

Some boys, especially town boys, are very much afraid of bees, but as a rule, except on very hot days, bees are too busy to sting. If anyone gets in the way of their flight, as when standing peering down at a hive when they are coming out, they sometimes sting then. In certain weather also, bees do get irritable, and at such times it is best to leave the hive alone for a day or two.

When working with bees, do everything quietly and fearlessly; do not give the hive a sudden knock or jar, and when removing sections, as explained later, take care not to do anything with a jerk. In any case, a bee sting is practically never serious with a healthy person.

To subdue the bees, a smoker is used. Besides a smoker, a novice should wear a veil and gloves. An experienced bee-farmer, however, can usually dispense with the veil and gloves; after practice in handling the sections etc., apparently, the farmer gets inoculated against bee stings after the first one or two, and he experiences no inconvenience from them. Should he, however, still experience pain from the stings, he should continue to wear the veil and gloves when working with the bees.

Feeding: If after a swarm has been put into a new hive, the weather is wet and cold for two or three days, the bees will not be able to collect food. Also, in winter, it is sometimes necessary to feed them.

All the surplus honey should be removed before the end of August, and the brooding chambers – that is the frames in the under part of the hives – should be carefully examined to see if the queen is all right, and also to see if there is a sufficient stock of food to carry the bees over the winter months. Feeding should never be done during winter months; if possible, not later than the beginning of September. Twenty-five pounds of honey is necessary in an average hive to be safe.

Swarming: The reason for swarming is not definitely known, but it is probably owing to the increased population of the hive.

The bees do not swarm in cold or wet weather, and only when the hive is well stocked with eggs.

The start of the swarming season is when the milder weather of spring comes on, and on a bright day. It occasionally happens that bees who appear to have made up their minds to swarm on a bright day, retire quietly to the old hive if the sun is suddenly obscured by a cloud.

Bees, as a rule, give every indication of their intention to swarm. They cluster idly outside of the hives in large numbers, for days, and even weeks, before they decide to migrate. The queen gets restless, and this seems to communicate itself to the workers. They can be seen hurrying aimlessly to and fro in the combs with seeming impatience. A general buzz is heard throughout the hive from time to time, and the workers are busy storing up food in their bodies.

On the day the swarm leaves, the workers do not go any distance from the hive. Suddenly, all noise is hushed and all the bees enter the hive; this is a sign that the swarming is about to take place. A few workers appear at the door, and striking with their wings, apparently give the signal for flight.

All those who are going, swarm to the door and hover over the hive until all are massed together, then, having selected a rallying point, generally a tree or bush, they all cluster onto it.

When a queen leaves the hive, or disappears, the bees do not at first notice anything, but, left in the hive after an hour or so, they discover their loss, and fly about in all directions looking for her. If they cannot find her, they liberate one of the young queens, or if there are none, they proceed to hatch out a new grub. First, they make a royal cell by knocking down the walls of three or four cells, and killing the grubs in them. They then feed up a young grub with special food – royal jelly – which makes it grow quickly.

Bees cannot exist in a close or impure atmosphere. To ventilate the hive, some of the bees fasten themselves to the floor of the hive, and by the rapid vibration of their wings as when flying, a powerful current of air is propelled through the hive.

BIRD WARDEN BADGE

In his own district, with regard to bird life in general, the Scout must know:

(a) The chief natural dangers (animal, bird etc.) to which they are exposed, and how to prevent their depredation; (b) Any social customs, ideas or superstitions that threaten their existence; (c) Any laws passed, or practical steps taken, to protect them.

Must have a practical knowledge of the construction of three different types of nest boxes for different species of birds, and how they should be used to best advantage.

Must have fed birds in his district for at least one year by means of food houses, food tables or food sticks.

Must produce a notebook of, and be familiar with, the habits, calls and appearances of at least twelve distinct varieties of birds in his district.

Must have kept records of birds and nests in his district for over a year, giving such particulars as: Registered number; Species of bird; Date when first seen or heard; Date of finding nest; Kind of tree, or bush, or tussock. Height above ground; Number of eggs or young; Date of leaving nest; Remarks.

The earning of this Badge should be the means of spending some of the happiest hours of your life. There are books from which you can learn the chief natural dangers that Birds are exposed to, but the book that you can learn most from is the book that Nature has always open in her lap for you to read. The pages she spreads for your eyes to read in fields and woodlands are some days sunlit and some days grey and misty. She has stories to tell you at dawn, at dusk, at night and all through the day. You have read of the dangers that beset the birds from cat and fox, stoat or weasel. You have known for some time that the barn owl's nightly feast is not confined to mice, that the hawk every now and then swoops down to kill the lark. But have you asked yourself: how and when are these things done? Have you hunted the hunter, tracked the cat, seen the fox, laid low in the meadows and watched the hawk? Have you managed to borrow those field glasses and, lying well hidden, scouted at long range?

Are there snakes in your district? What other enemies have the birds besides? You do not want to learn from books – so you go out into the open at any time by day or night – and hunt for "possible enemies" – in other words, you act as soldiers act – suspecting everything that you have the slightest reason to suppose is not a "friend". You must not be disheartened if it takes time. The gamekeeper was not a gamekeeper in a day – he can tell you a lot if you offer to carry his cartridges and ask him questions. He will tell you things that are not written in books – things that belong to your district – the social customs and local ideas and superstitions that threaten the existence of the birds.

You can learn a great deal about birds by watching their nests and the way the young birds are brought up. It is often difficult to get near enough to the nest in its natural site to see the young birds fed or being taught to fly. If you make nest boxes you will be able to keep your birds under close observation. Nest boxes should represent the birds' natural home as much as possible and so, of course, they vary a great deal in construction. They have, as a rule, a weatherproof roof which can open and shut – so that, if you are very quiet and wary, you can peep in at the youngsters while the parents are away. There is always a round hole for the entrance and the box is covered outside with bark. The size of the hole is dependent on the size of the birds' natural nest. The boxes are hung up by a hook and you must know something about nests before you hang up your nest boxes in the spring – some birds build in trees, some in hedges, some at one height from the ground, some at another. If there is anything about your nest box that is wrong the wise little bird will be suspicious and your nest box will remain empty.

By watching your birds and listening to their song day after day, you will soon learn to know whether they are happy and free, or whether something is frightening them. To know the habits, calls, and appearances of birds, you must read books and then verify what you have read in the open spaces and woods. You must ask questions of the countrymen you meet in your rambles. Your notebook should have so many pages allotted to each variety of bird you are going to study, and your notes must be interesting, with little details, little incidents, to make them "alive".

BLACKSMITH BADGE

A Scout must be able to upset and weld a one-inch iron rod, make a horseshoe, know how to tire a wheel, use a sledgehammer and forge, and how to shoe and rough a horse correctly, and be able to temper iron and steel.

This is not an easy badge to get, and a Scout who wants it must be instructed by a practical man, and, of course, must procure the use of a fire and tools from some smith. So for this badge it is best for Scoutmasters to form a class, and then get the local blacksmith to take them in hand.

Upset and Weld a One-Inch Iron Bar

Upsetting a bar is the process usually adopted when it is required to render the bar a little thicker at some portion of its length. For instance, if the portion to be upset is at the extreme end, a "short heat" is taken. That means that the extreme end is made white hot, and then instantly thrust down or "jumped" on the anvil several times; or it is stood on the anvil with the cold end uppermost, and the latter struck forcibly until the desired effect is produced Fig. 1 (a) and (b)

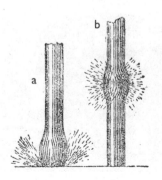

Fig. I.

Fig. 2.

shows where the heat has been taken at a point distant from the extremity. The procedure is the same.

To weld a bar, the ends are first drawn out till they are tapered for about 3 or 4 inches, so that they form a scarf joint. Each piece is then brought to a welding heat and a little sand strewed on each. Welding heat is known by the iron beginning to burn with vivid sparks. When this heat is reached, the pieces must be quickly taken from the fire, the sand dusted on, and the ends placed together on the anvil and joined by several quick sharp blows of the hammer. As the smith has only two hands, he requires an assistant, who takes the one piece, while the smith takes the other and the hammer.

The Horseshoe

The horseshoe generally has the same shape, but varies in size according to the animal for which it is intended, so the piece of bar iron from which it is made may vary from 7 inches in length to 14 or 15 inches, and in width from ¾ inch to 1¼ inches, and in thickness from 3/8 inch to 5/8 inch.

According to the principle upon which ordinary smiths make a show for a full-grown horse, it is ½ inch thick at the toe, but near the heel 3/8 inch thick. At the tow it is an inch wide and continues round to the quarters, lessening away towards the heel, where it is ½ inch wide (see Fig. 2).

The heated iron is first forged to the usual circular shape, and then the groove which runs round a great portion of the shoe is formed by means of a fullering or grooving tool. When this is done the nail holes are punched (generally seven) in the groove. The "clip" at the toe is then turned up on the edge of the anvil. Lastly, another heat is taken at the heel of the shoe, and the "caulkens", or elevated heels, are turned up if required. This is usually done on the edge of the anvil, but some farriers employ a tool specially made for it. "Caulkens", although generally on the hind shoes in many parts for hard work, are by no means universally in favour, and are never necessary on the large shoes of plough horses.

Fig. 3 (a) shows a horseshoe for heavy work, while Fig. 3 (b) shows an improved form of shoe (a) being the upper or foot surface, (b) the under or ground surface.

Use a sledge hammer and forge: how to do this cannot be described, and must be learned in the smithy itself.

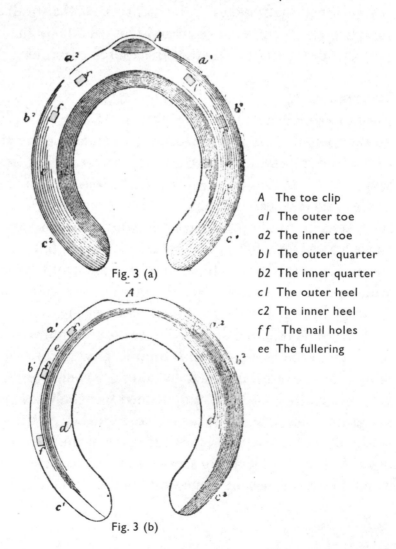

Fig. 3 (a)

Fig. 3 (b)

A   The toe clip
a1 The outer toe
a2 The inner toe
b1 The outer quarter
b2 The inner quarter
c1 The outer heel
c2 The inner heel
f f   The nail holes
ee The fullering

BOATMAN BADGE

A Scout Must:

Be able to manage a boat single-handed, rowing, punting, and sculling over the stern.

Be able to steer a boat under oars and bring her alongside a vessel and landing stage.

Must be able to box the compass.

Know how to tow or be towed.

Must be able to distinguish the various classes of vessels by their rig.

Must be able to make the various bends and hitches, knots and splices, and be able to throw a line.

Rowing

The great mistake usually made in rowing is doing the pulling entirely with the arms. A person who rows with his arms alone very soon gets tired, power is lost, the elbows are stuck out at right angles at the finish of the stroke, and the oar is pushed too low in the water. The arms should play a very little part in rowing; the legs, back and shoulders should do most of the work.

Sit square in the boat, have the stretcher as near to the body as is comfortable, keep the heels together, feet at an angle of 45 to each other, and keep the back straight. Grasp the oar with the two upper joints of the fingers, thumb underneath the oar. Grip the oar firmly, but not as if squeezing it. The lower part of the palm of the hand and the ball of the thumb should not touch the oar at all. Gripping the oar in this way, the possibility of cramp is minimised and the wrists have free play.

It is difficult to put in writing exactly how the stroke is made. If the Scout can get a good oarsman to sit in front of him, in order that he can copy his movements, he will quickly be able to row properly. The main points to remember are: not to row with the arms; to bring the oar straight out of the water at the end of the stroke; and to feather smartly by turning the wrist, when the blade is clear of the water. The oar should always be kept on the same plane – that is to say, it should be at the same depth throughout the stroke under the water, and at the same height above the water on being brought back for the next stroke.

A tenderfoot is easily noticed in a boat. He pulls entirely with his arms, and, therefore, his oar is alternately high in the air, and deep in the water, making almost a complete circle with each stroke. Let arms and body work together like machinery. Never jerk; smoothness and steadiness are essential.

Sculling

Is the art of moving a boat along by means of only one oar.

The person who is going to scull should stand with his feet firmly placed on the bottom boards in the after part of the boat and be facing towards the stern. Launch the oar over the stern, place it in the rowlock and bring it over to the port side of the boat, then incline the blade so that it will cut the water at an angle of about 30 degrees, and, in that manner, pull it over to the opposite side. When finishing the stroke, give the oar a half turn so as to bring the blade back again at the same angle and in such a manner that the edge of the blade that was uppermost in the first stroke is brought underneath in the back stroke. Continue to bring the oar backwards and forwards in this manner and it will be found that the boat will go ahead almost straight, providing that the angle which the blade forms with the water is the same on both strokes. It will be noticed by those who understand the action of a steamer's propeller, that the movement of the oar just described is, in a less scientific degree, the same as that of the blades of the propeller.

Towing

When towing another boat, make a bowline in her painter and secure it by passing it up between the two after thwarts and reeving a stretcher through it to act as a toggle.

When towed by another boat, or a ship, secure the two lines in the same way between the two foremost thwarts, or make a bowline in the end of your painter and reeve the painter under a stretcher between the two foremost thwarts and pass the bowline into the towing boat, the other end of the painter remaining stacked in its proper place. In both cases have a man standing by ready to ship.

On Running before a Broken Sea, or Surf, to the Shore

The following general rules may therefore be depended on when running before, or attempting to land through, a heavy surf or broken water.

As far as possible avoid each sea by placing the boat where the sea will break ahead or astern of her.

If the sea be very heavy, or if the boat by very small, and especially if she have a square stern, bring her bow round to seaward and back her in, rowing ahead against each heavy surf to allow it to pass the boat.

If it be considered safe to proceed to the shore bow foremost, back the oars against each sea on its approach, so as to stop the boat's way through the water as far as possible, and, if there is a drogue or any other instrument in the boat which may be used as one, tow it astern to aid in keeping the boat end-on to the sea, which is the chief object in view.

Bring the principal weights in the boat towards the end that is to seaward, but not to the extreme end.

If a boat worked by both sails and oars be running under

sail for the land through a heavy sea, her crew should, under all circumstances, unless the beach be quite steep, take down her masts and sails before entering the broken water, and take her to land under oars alone, as above described. If she have sails only, her sails should be much reduced, a half-lowered foresail or other small headsail being sufficient.

Rigs of Vessels

The following sketches will enable the student to recognise the rigs far better than a long description of each would.

Starting at the smallest of our seagoing ailing vessels, we have the sloop or cutter, which is generally used by pilots, on account of the handiness of the rig, which enables one man to handle it after the sails are once set.

A schooner may be of any number of masts, but the most

CUTTER or SLOOP
1. The mainsail.   2. The gaff topsail.   3. The foresail.   4. The jib.

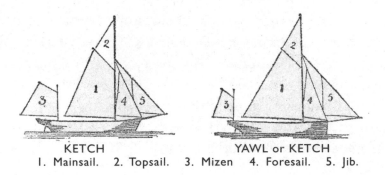

KETCH
1. Mainsail.   2. Topsail.   3. Mizen   4. Foresail.   5. Jib.

YAWL or KETCH

common around our coasts are the two – and three – masted ones. They are easily recognised by nearly all their sails setting fore and aft, like the mainsail in the sloop; the only exception being in what is known as the topsail schooner, and then the topsails on the foremast are set on yards attached to the foremast, which, by means of tackles, known as braces, are made fast to the end of the yard, and can be hauled around to suit the wind.

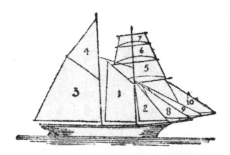

TOPSAIL SCHOONER

THREE-MASTED SCHOONER

1. Forsail.	7. Fore topgallant sail.
2. Stay foresail.	8. Inner jib
3. Mainsail	9. Outer jib.
4. Mainsail.	10. Flying jib.
5. Fore lower topsail.	11. Mizen trysail.
6. Fore upper topsail.	12. Mizen topsail.

The brigantine is very much like, and often mistaken for, a topsail schooner, but, as is shown in the sketch, there is a decided difference between the two. It will be noticed when studying the sketch of a schooner that the lowest sail on the foremast is set fore-and-aft; whereas, the corresponding sail in the brigantine is a square sail, which allows additional staysails in the brigantine is a square sail, which allows additional staysails to be set between the masts.

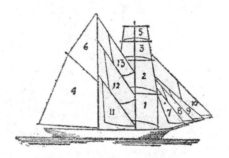

BRIGANTINE

1. Forsail.	7. Fore topmast staysail.
2. Fore topsail.	8. Inner jib.
3. Fore topgallant sail.	9. Outer jib.
4. Mainsail.	10. Flying jib.
5. Fore royal.	11. Main staysail.
6. Main topsail.	12. Main topmast staysail.
	13. Main topgallant staysail.

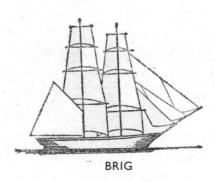

BRIG

Splicing Ropes

An Eye Splice is formed by unlaying the end of a rope for a short distance, and then, after closing up the end, to form an eye of the desired size. Lay the three strands upon the standing part, now tuck the middle strand through the strand of the standing part of the rope next to it (against the lay of the rope), then pass the strand on the left over the strands under which No. 1 strand is tucked, and tuck it under the next, and, lastly, put the remaining strand through the third strand on the other side of the rope (Fig. 1). Now tuck each strand again alternately over a strand and under a strand of rope, and then taper off by halving the strands before tucking the third time, and again halve them before the fourth tuck.

If the strands are tucked with the lay of the rope it is termed a Sailmakers' Splice.

Fig. I.

A Short Splice is used to join two ropes when it is not required to pass through a block. Unlay the two ropes the required distance, and clutch them together as in Fig. 2 (overleaf), that is, so that the stands of one rope go alternately between the strands of the other.

Then tuck the strands of rope *a* into the rope *b* in similar manner to that described in an Eye Splice, and similarly tuck the strands of *b* into *a* (Figs. 3 and 4, below).

Fig. 2.

A Cut Splice is made by laying two ropes in the position indicated in Fig. 4.

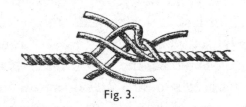

Fig. 3.

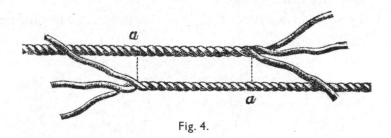

Fig. 4.

Leaving the ropes between *a a* to form an oblong loop, tuck the strands of one rope into the other, as done in the Eye Splice. Splices are often wormed, parceled, and served. Fig. 5 shows the Cut Splice after this treatment.

A Log-Line Splice is a Cut Splice, but, instead of allowing the loop to appear, the two lines are twisted together (Fig. 5).

Fig. 5.

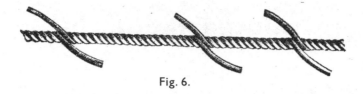

Fig. 6.

A Long Splice is one of the most useful of splices, as it permits the rope to run through a block just the same as an unspliced rope. Unlay the ends of two ropes to a distance about four times the length used in a Short Splice, and then clutch them together as if about to commence a Short Splice. Now, unlay one strand for a considerable distance and fill up the gap thus caused by twisting in the strand opposite to it of the other rope. Then, do the same with two more strands. Let the remaining two strands stay as they were first placed. The ropes will now appear as in Fig. 6 (above). To finish off, tuck the ends as in a Short Splice, but with the lay of the rope – that is, so that the tuck will continually take place around the same strand, and taper off gradually by reducing the yarns in the strand.

To make a Grommet: cut a strand about three and a half times the length of the grommet required. Unlay the rope carefully, and keep the turns of the strand in. Close up the strand in the form of a ring (Fig. 7), and then pass the ends round and round in their original lay until all the intervals are filled up (Fig. 8), and then finish off the two ends as in a Long Splice (Fig. 9).

Fig. 7.   Fig. 8.   Fig. 9.

BUGLER BADGE

A Scout must be able to sound properly on the bugle the
Scout's Rally and the following Army calls: Alarm, Charge,
Orderlies (ord. corpls.), Orders, Warning for Parade, Quarter Bugle,
Fall in, Dismiss, Rations, 1st and 2nd Dinner calls (men's),
Reveille, Last Post, Lights out.

The Scouts' Call (no. 1) should precede each of the other calls.

1. Scouts' Call.

2. Charge.

3. Alarm.

4. Orderly Corporals.

5. Orders.

6. Warning for Parade.

7. Quarter Call.

8. Fall In.

9. No Parade (or Dismiss).

10. Rations.

11. Men's Meal (1st Call).

11. Men's Meal (2nd Call).

13. Reveille.

14. Tattoo (Last Post).

15. Lights Out.

CAMPER BADGE

A Scout must:

1. Have camped out 30 nights, taking an active part in the work of the camp, either in bivouac or under canvas, or on board ship or boat.

2. Know what minimum requisites in (a) kit, (b) utensils, (c) rations are required for seven boys for a week's camp or cruise, and have cooked all meals for them for three days, not necessarily consecutive.

3. Demonstrate what kit he would take on a tramping trek or bicycling trek or sea cruise and have taken part in one of these for not less than three days, covering at least nine miles a day.

4. Know how to select and lay out a camp for (a) a patrol, (b) a troop 40 strong, making necessary kitchens, rubbish pits, latrines, etc.; or know how o select an anchorage; mooring or berth for (a) a rowing or sailing vessel, (b) a sea-going vessel.

5. Demonstrate that (a) he understands the use and care of an axe, (b) has a knowledge of knots and he understands lashings.

6. Demonstrate how to pitch and strike a tent capable of holding seven Scouts, and carry out ordinary repairs to same.

7. Build a shelter for three Scouts using only natural materials, or a boat's sail and spars, or make a suitable patrol tent of any old material.

The tests for this badge can only be passed by practical experience.

There are two different styles of camping necessary, namely (1) a standing camp – that is to say, camping on one spot for several days at a time; (2) a trek camp, where the camping ground is changed daily. The field kitchen and sanitary arrangements would, of course, each be different.

There is no use giving here full details regarding camping. The subject is very fully treated in *Scouting for Boys* by the Chief Scout. The following points should, however, be emphasised:

(1) a "daily routine" should be drawn up and must be strictly kept. Nothing spoils a camp so much as slackness in this respect.

(2) Absolute quietness between "lights out" and "reveille".

(3) Daily airing of tent and bedding. The tent flaps should be rolled up first thing in the morning in fine weather and everything taken out of the tent and arranged tidily outside. The tent should be cleaned out, and all papers, straw and refuse collected and burned daily. Refuse which will not burn should be buried.

Cleanliness and tidiness should be the watchword.

A camp ground very soon gets dirty if careful attention is not paid to this.

Kit for seven boys for a week: Tent, lantern, candles, matches, mallet, spare pegs, tin basin, spade, axe, pole strap, stew pot, frying pan, kettle, bucket, pail, butcher's knife, ladle, dishcloths, cleaning rags, bags for potatoes etc., large tins for biscuits, bread etc., jugs for milk.

Each individual should have a waterproof sheet, blankets (two or more, according to the season and locality), sufficient in any case to enable each Scout to have a separate bed.

In addition to full Scout's uniform, each individual should have: greatcoat, two flannel shirts, two pairs of stockings, pair of drawers, sleeping suit, extra pair of strong boots or shoes, pair of canvas shoes, sweater, hairbrush, housewife, towel and soap, toothbrush and powder, handkerchiefs, haversack, billy, staff, knife, fork, spoon, mug, dishes.

First-aid equipment: Clinical thermometer; roller bandages with different widths, gauze, lint, boracic lint, triangular bandages, cotton wool; tincture of iodine; disinfectant such as Lysol; court plaster, strapping plaster; picric acid for burns; ammonia for stings, etc.; boracic ointment, lanoline; ammoniated quinine; cascara sagrada, Epsom or other salts; scissors, safety pins, needles and tweezers for extracting thorns and splinters.

Latrines: Should be at least 100 yards to the leeward of camp. A trench 3 feet by $1^1/2$ feet, and $1^1/2$ feet deep, surrounded by a canvas screen.

When digging the trench, the turf should be kept to be replaced later.

Loose earth available, to be put in the trench after use, and a small shovel. The trench should be sprinkled night and morning with chloride of lime. Toilet paper in sheets should be kept in a tin or box. Old newspapers should never be used.

A separate urinal trench should be provided, also a urinal trench nearer the tents for night use only.

It should be impressed on the boys that the latrines must be kept clean and in proper order.

Choosing second-hand tents: Undoubtedly, by far the best tents are made of Russian flax, but, since the war started, practically none of this flax has been imported.

Never buy a second-hand tent without examining it. Tents with small holes are a constant source of worry.

Old tents which have been waterproofed are most unhealthy as there is no ventilation through the canvas. Tents made of specially waterproofed material are different, because then the yarn has been waterproofed – not the whole tent.

Pitching bell tents: Team of five. Of course, experienced campers can do with less.

Put in a peg where the centre of tent is to be. Measure a pole length from centre to each corner (see figure) and put in pegs.

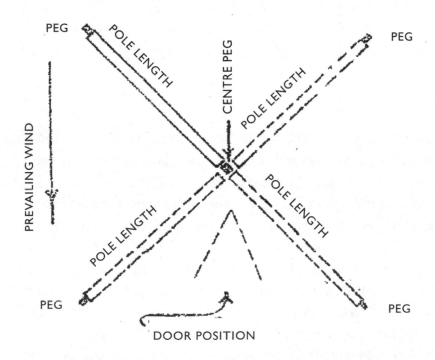

Unroll tent, the bottom of tent to be at centre, the rest of the tent lying door uppermost on the side of the centre peg further from the side where the door is to be. Lace up door.

The corner or main guys, usually coloured red, are next

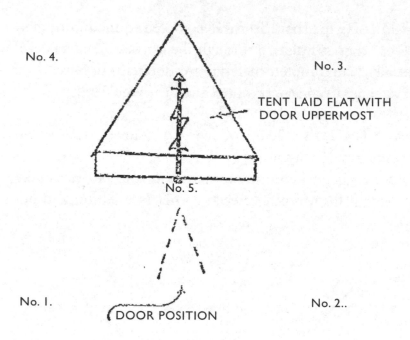

No. 4.

No. 3.

TENT LAID FLAT WITH
DOOR UPPERMOST

No. 5.

No. 1.

DOOR POSITION

No. 2..

unloosened. (All others should be left unrolled meantime.) If the main guys are not coloured, numbering from the door round by the right the main guys are 3, 7, 11, 15.

Four of the pitching team stand at the pegs, the fifth taking the pole. No. 5 inserts the pole, making sure that it fits exactly and firmly into the cap. When ready, he calls, "hoist," 1 and 2 pull on the guys, 3 and 4 put sufficient strain on to prevent the tent going too far forward. The four main guys are then put on the pegs. No. 5 inside the tent directs those at the main guys to tighten or loosen, as the case may be, until the tent stands square. If the pole is not exactly in the cap, the tent must be lowered, as no correction of the guys can put it properly home.

The rest of the guys are now unrolled and the pegs hammered in. Care should be taken to see that the pegs make a perfect circle, and that the seams of the tent and the guy ropes to the pegs are in a perfectly straight line. Considerable alteration will be required before this is accomplished, and the pegs will require attention daily, as the tent gets slewed around in wet, dewy or windy weather.

Care of tents in camp: Never put any nails in the pole. Never touch the canvas when wet – a shower bath for the occupants is the result. At night, see that everything – boots, kitbag, bedding etc. – is quite clear of the side of the tent. Anything touching the canvas will be soaked through in the morning, by dew in fine weather, rain in wet.

Striking bell tents: Take out all pegs and place them in the peg bag. Take out all guys, except the four main guys, roll up the guys tightly, finishing off with two half-hitches.

As with pitching tents, there should be a team of five.

When all but the main guys are rolled, stand to the main guys. When No. 5 says, "Ready," remove the main guys and hold them tight. On the command, "Strike," No. 5 lowers the pole backwards, Nos. 3 and 4 run forward, with guy ropes fully taut, thus pulling the back of the tent under the pole. Remove the pole. Roll up the main guys and remove the pegs. Fasten the door, take each side of the tent and turn it into the centre, fold once again into the centre, and once again. Roll tightly from the cap. The tent will then fit into the bag.

Never strike a tent when wet, even with dew – put off striking as long as possible. If it is necessary to strike a wet tent, see that it is taken out and dried at once on return home.

CARPENTER BADGE

A Scout must be able to shute and glue a 2-ft straight joint, make a housing, tenon and mortice, and halved joint, grind and set a chisel and plane iron, make a dovetailed locked box, or a table or chair.

The jack plane is used for general work, and the smoothing plane only for finishing.

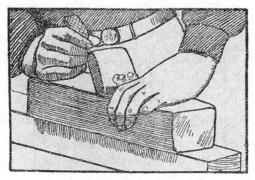

THE JACK PLANE.

The rip saw is used for "ripping," that is for cutting parallel to the grain of the wood, and for cross-cutting. The tenon saw is used only for fine cross-cutting.

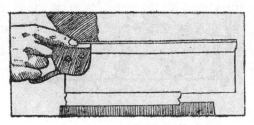

THE TENON SAW.

THE RIP SAW.

It is almost impossible to explain in writing the correct way to use each tool. Practical instruction from an experienced carpenter, either amateur or professional, is the best way to learn.

The correct method of using the rip and tenon saws, and jack, is shown above.

The chief point to guard against in sawing, is using the saw at too great an angle, thus making too long a cut, and bending the saw to or from the body if it tends to run out of its course. In the latter case the proper way to turn the saw is to twist it slightly by the handle on the downstroke, keeping the blade of the saw straight. The forefinger of the right hand should be kept outside of the handle, and thus assist in guiding the saw. It is impossible to cut straight unless the blade is kept quite vertical at each part of the stroke. A Scout should therefore study to avoid describing an arc of a circle with the hand and arm, thus bending the saw on both the up and down strokes.

With the plane, beginners should try to avoid sending the plane in a circular manner. Each stroke should be straight, not curved. How to hold the plane is shown in the illustration opposite.

CLERK BADGE

A Scout must have the following qualifications:
Have good handwriting and hand-printing.
Ability to use a typewriting machine.
Ability to write a letter from memory on the subject given verbally five
    minutes previously.
Knowledge of simple book-keeping.
Or, as an alternative to Typewriting –
Write in shorthand from dictation at twenty words a minute as minimum.

Book-keeping: Book-keeping is the art of keeping a correct record of one's business transactions with a view to being able at any time to ascertain the exact position of one's affairs – one's assets and liabilities; and whether a profit or loss has been made.

The best system, and the one most commonly in use, is the Double Entry System, the fundamental principle of which is that every transaction must be entered twice, once on the debit side and once on the credit side of the ledger, so that if the books are correct, the total of both sides will be the same. The reason for this is that every transaction involves two parties – the giver and receiver.

Many different books are used, which vary according to the nature of the business – but those which are absolutely necessary and which are yet sufficient are – cash book, journal and ledger.

Cash Book: This does not need much explanation. As the name implies, it is used for all transactions involving the transference of cash. The left-hand side of each folio is used for receipts, and the right-hand side for payments.

Thus, if £20 is received from Tom Jones, and £10 paid to John Jackson, the entries would be as under:

Dr.		CASH					CONTRA		CR.		
			£	S.	D.						
Nov.	7	To Tom Jones	20	0	0	Nov.	10	By John Jackson	10	0	0

The single column to the left of the money columns is used for the ledger folio when the amount is posted to that book. This will be explained when dealing with the ledger.

Journal: All transactions except the receiving and payment of cash go through this book – or a similar one answering the same purpose – which, unlike the cash book, has the debit and credit columns alongside one another on the same page. The purpose of this book is to prepare entries for the ledger, and the method of procedure is as following:

Suppose that A. sells goods value £10 to B., and pays the forwarding charges £1 on B.'s account. The entry would be B. debtor £11 (which would go in the debit column); in the next line, Goods A/c creditor £10 (in the credit column); and in the next line Charges A/c creditor £1 (also in the credit column). Thus:

				Dr.			CR.		
				£	S.	D.	£	S.	D.
Nov.	3	Mr. B.	Dr.	11					
			To Goods A/c Cr.						
			To Charges A/c Cr.						

It will be seen that the debits (or the sum of the debits) are equal to the credits (or the sum of the credits), and this must be the case with every journal entry.

As in the cash book, there is a column for the ledger folio.

Ledger: This is the most important book, containing, as it does, extracts of all the entries in the cash book and journal, and giving the ultimate information for which all books are kept. It contains the separate accounts of all the different firms and individuals with whom we have dealings, and, in addition, goods, charges and any other accounts which the special nature of the business makes necessary. These accounts have each a debit and a credit side, which are the left- and right-hand pages of the folio, respectively, and the entries in the cash book and journal are posted here. These last-mentioned books are called Books of Original Entry, as all the entries go through either one or other of them before being posted to the ledger.

Dr.		CASH						CONTRA	Cr.		
			£	S.	D.						
Nov.	7	To Tom Jones	20	0	0	Nov.	10	By John Jackson	10	0	0

Trial Balance: To ascertain if the books are correct, the balances from the different ledger accounts are taken, and if the sum of the debit balances is equal to the sum of the credit balances, it shows that double entry has been carried out, and, so far as this is concerned, the books are correct.

Balance Sheet: To find the financial position at the end of a certain period, a balance sheet is drawn up. On one side are put the liabilities, which consist of capital, and the various sums the firm owes to others, while on the other side are placed the assets, consisting of property, stock and the amounts owing to the firm by others. The excess of assets over liabilities is the profit, but if the liabilities are the greater there is a loss.

While the foregoing shows in a general way the mode of procedure with a few simple entries, it must be borne in mind that, in practice, all businesses have different ways of applying the principles of book-keeping. However, the principles as exemplified do not vary to any extent, and, if they are thoroughly understood, no great difficulty should be experienced in adapting them to the books of any ordinary business.

Business letters should be started as follows:
Messrs. James Brown & Son,
Glasgow.
Dear Sirs (or Gentlemen),

   And finished –
   Yours truly
   (or Yours faithfully)
   John Black & Co.

The envelope should be addressed:
Messrs. James Brown & Son,
52 Darnley Street,
Pollokshields,
Glasgow.

Forms of addressing persons of rank:
THE BRITISH SOVEREIGN.
   Begin: Sir (or Madam).
      End: I remain,
      With profoundest veneration,
      Sir (or Madam),
      Your Majesty's most faithful Subject,
      and dutiful Servant.
   Superscribe (direct):
      To the King's (or Queen's) Most Excellent Majesty.

THE PRINCE (OR PRINCESS) OF WALES.
Begin: Sir (or Madam).
    End: I remain,
    With the greatest respect,
    Sir (or Madam),
    You Royal Highness's most dutiful, most
    Humble, and most devoted Servant.
 Superscribe:
    To His Royal Highness the Prince of Wales.
    To Her Royal Highness the Princess of Wales.

PRINCESS ROYAL, PRINCES AND PRINCESSES OF
THE BLOOD ROYAL.
Begin: Madam (or Sir).
    End: I remain, Madam (or Sir), Your Royal
    Highness's most humble and obedient Servant.
Superscribe:
    To Her Royal Highness the Princess Royal; or to His
    Royal Highness the Duke of C____; or To Her Royal
    Highness the Duchess of C____; or to His (or Her)
    Royal Highness Prince E____ (or Princess B____).

Nobility:
DUKES.
Begin: My Lord Duke.
    End: I remain, my Lord Duke,
    Your Graces most obedient Servant.
Superscribe:
    To His Grace the Duke of A____, K.T. etc.

MARQUISES.
Begin: My Lord Marquis.
  End: as to a Duke, with Lordship in place of Grace.
  Superscribe: To the Most Honourable the Marquis of
  Salisbury, K.G. etc.

EARLS, VISCOUNTS, AND BARONS.
Begin: My Lord.
  End: As to a Marquis.
Superscribe:
  To the Right Honourable The Earl of Rosebery, K. T,;
  or to The Right Honourable The Lord Viscount
  Cranbrook; or to The Right Honourable Lord
  Coleridge, D. C. L.

BARONETS AND KNIGHTS.
Begin: Sir.
  End: I remain, Sir, Your most obedient Servant.
Superscribe:
  Sir George O___ T___, Bart., G.C,S.I.; or Sir James
  B____, L.L.D. etc.

Note:

WIVES OF DUKES.
Madam. I remain, Madam, Your Grace's most obedient
Servant. To her Grace the Duchess of A____.

WIVES OF MARQUISES.
Madam. I remain, Madam, Your Ladyship's most
obedient Servant. Superscribe: To the Most Honourable
the Marchioness of S___.

WIVES OF EARLS, VISCOUNTS AND BARONS.
Begin and end as to a Marchioness.
Superscribe: The Right Honourable the Countess of
B____; or the Right Honourable the Lady Viscountess
____; or The Right Honourable Lady ____.

WIVES OF BARONETS AND KNIGHTS.
Madam. I remain, Madam, Your most obedient Servant.
Superscribe: Lady H____.
see p.77, 3up, for example.

Typewriting: Ability to use a typewriting machine can really only be acquired after practice with one, and there is little that can be said about it here. As the keyboard, however, in nearly all typewriters is the same, anyone who learns the position of the various letters will find it easier to typewrite when the opportunity occurs for practicing with a machine.

The keyboard given is that of the Remington Typewriter Company, as being one of the standard makes. Some typewriters have a separate key for every character, capitals and small letters. In the keyboard given here, the letters are all small letters, and in order to print a capital it is necessary to strike the shift key and keep this down while striking the letter required. In order to strike the top character in those keys having two character, the shift key must be used in the same manner.

In order to practise typing, copy out the keyboard given here on a much larger scale on a separate piece of paper, and then practise by striking the keys lightly with the tips of the fingers. In operating, use three fingers of each hand, striking the right and left half of the keyboard with the right and left hands, respectively. Beware of the one-finger method, and practise using three fingers of each hand from the beginning, as a higher speed of typing is attained in the end. In practicing writing with the dummy keyboard, remember always at the end of each word to strike the space key so as to separate the various words from each other.

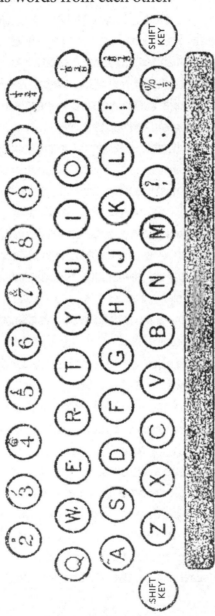

COAST WATCHMAN BADGE

A Scout must know every rock and shoal within the five-fathom line on a four mile stretch of coast near his headquarters. He must know the rise and fall of tides, both spring and neap, and how to ascertain the times of high and low water. He must know when the moon rises or sets and its quarter. He must know the set of the currents at all times of tide. He must know all danger spots to bathers and visitors, such as quicksands and places where they are liable to be cut off by the tide, and what to do if they get into difficulties. He must know the best landing-places for boats and where they can find shelter in bad weather. He must know the marks of fishing boats which frequent the coast and the national flags of ships which pass. He must know the lighthouses which can be seen from his strip of coast and describe the lights they exhibit. He must know the beacons, storm signals, coastguard stations, steam tugs, lifeboats and rocket apparatus, the nearest telegraph offices, telephones and addresses of doctors available from each point and the mercantile code of signals.

The knowledge required to obtain this badge cannot be given fully for every port in this article, as each place will have local peculiarities which can only be learned by careful observation and continued perseverance; but, by explaining where the information may be found, it will put you on the right track and probably save a lot of time.

In the first place, you must spend a lot of your time on the coast and carefully watch the various peculiarities of the tides. You will be able to tell the way the tide is running by watching any vessel that is at anchor, and she will nearly always be heading in the direction from which the tide is flowing, the only exception being in the case of a ship that is light; if the wind is very strong she may be heading towards the wind. Or you can see the water swirling away from a buoy. When a chance presents itself, make friends with some of the fishermen or coastguards who will be able, from their experience, to tell you a lot of useful information regarding their stretch of coast.

Then to be perfectly familiar with the position, size and shape of rocks and shoals it would be advisable to obtain a plan chart, which can be bought from any nautical opticians. The reason for buying a chart is that in the five-fathom limit there will probably be some rocks or shoals which are never exposed to view, as it must be remembered that five fathom is 30 feet.

The five-fathom limit will be marked on the chart by dots in groups of fives, thus ….. ….. ….. and all the signs and abbreviations used on the chart will be found in the title space, and the abbreviations used on all charts will be found under the Pilot's Badge.

Notes on tides: The rise and fall of the tide, together with the high water, full and change, will also be found on the chart. If you require to find the time of high water for any day, go to any almanac which contains the phases of the moon, and see when it was new or full moon, count up the number of days that have elapsed since the mean of the two phases mentioned, and to the time of high water, full and change, add 48 minutes for each of the days, and that will give approximately the afternoon tide for the day. Allow twelve hours twenty-four minutes back from your afternoon tide and you will have a rough idea of the morning tide.

Tides are chiefly due to the moon's attraction. As the earth revolves, the moon draws the water towards her, and as each place comes, as it were, beneath, or abreast of her, she raises the sea surface and causes high water. At the same moment, it is also high water on the opposite side of the earth, because the moon tends to attract the solid body of the earth away from the water, thus causing a raised wave there also.

Storm Signals: The uniform method in the British Isles during the daytime for signalling the approach of strong winds or storms is done by means of two cones, which are 3 feet in height and 3 feet wide at their base, and when they are viewed from a distance will appear in the form of a triangle.

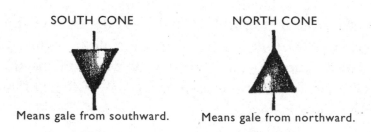

SOUTH CONE   NORTH CONE

Means gale from southward.   Means gale from northward.

The wind is said to "Veer" in the northern hemisphere when it shifts with the hands of a watch, and is said to "Back" when it shifts in the opposite direction or against the hands of a watch.

The South Cone is hoisted when strong winds or gales are expected from the S.E., veering to S.W., W. or N.W.; from S.W. veering to W. or N.W.; from W. veering to N.W., and also from E. veering to S. or S.W.

The North Cone is hoisted when strong winds or gales are expected from S.E., E. or N.E. backing to N.; from N.W.

veering N., N.E. or E., from N., veering to N.E. or E.; and also, from N.E. veering to E.

At night time when the cone can no longer be seen, it may be hauled down to save wear and tear.

The particular reason the authorities have had for hoisting up the signal will usually be found in some conspicuous place on a telegraph form sent to them by the Meteorological Office. The signal will be kept flying until 8 p.m. on the day following the receipt of the telegram, unless another telegram is received in the meantime stating "lower", which will mean that the danger is over. If required to keep it flying longer than the regulation time, a telegram will be received stating "keep up".

Rocket Apparatus: There are hard-and-fast rules laid down for the guidance of seamen regarding the use of Rocket Apparatus for saving life, in case of shipwreck on our coast, which you would be well advised to commit to memory from the Instructions Issued by the Board of Trade for the Guidance of Masters and Seamen when using the Rocket Apparatus for Saving Life.

The Mercantile Code of Signals: The flags which are those used in the Mercantile Marine, must be committed to memory and you must be able to recognise them at a distance. A bare knowledge of the flags is of very little use unless you know where to find their meaning, as it is very seldom that each flag hoisted represents its particular letter in a word.

In connection with the flags is published a book which gives the meaning of a certain combination of flags, and in this way a lot of time and trouble is saved, as a two, three, or four flag signal may, and usually does, indicate a whole sentence. The book is arranged in the simplest of forms, so that if you have the opportunity of handling one you will soon become familiar with it, and be able to pick out a signal or its meaning in a very short time.

The Code Flag over One Flag has a special meaning, and as there are only twenty-six of them they can easily be committed to memory and their meaning known without referring to the Signal Book. They are of an important character, so they are given here in full.

Urgent and Important Signals are Made with Two Flags

Code Flag over

A = "I am on full speed."

B = "I am taking in (or discharging)
　　　　gunpowder or other explosives."

C = "Yes," or Affirmative.

D = "No," or Negative

E = Alphabetical Signal No. 1.

F = 　　"　　　　"　No. 2.

G = 　　"　　　　"　No. 3.

H = "Stop," "Heave to," or "Come nearer," "Wish to communicate."

I = "I have not a clean bill of health."

J = "I have headway."

K = "I have sternway."

L = " I have (or have had) some dangerous infectious diseases on board."

M = Numeral Signal No. 1.

N = 　　"　　　　"　No. 2.

O = 　　"　　　　"　No. 3.

P = "I am about to sail."

Q = "I have a clean bill of health but am liable to quarantine."

R = "Do not pass ahead of me."

S=   "I want a pilot."

T = "Do not overtake me."

U = "My engines are stopped."

V = "My engines are going astern."

W = "All boats are returned to the ship."

X = "I will pass ahead of you."

Y = "All ships of the convoy are to rejoin company."

Z = "I will pass astern of you."

COOK BADGE

A Scout must be able to light a fire and make a cook-place with a few bricks or logs; cook the following dishes: Irish stew, vegetables, omelette, rice pudding, or any dishes which the examiner may consider equivalent; make tea, coffee, or cocoa; mix dough and bake bread in an oven; or a "damper" or "twist" (round stake) at a camp fire; carve properly, and hand plates and dishes correctly to people at table.

Porridge

Allow 1 pint of water for each person and 2 oz of coarse oatmeal, 1 teaspoon of salt. Bring the water to the boil, add the salt, sprinkle the oatmeal lightly into the water, stirring all the time. Let this simmer until it is cooked, not under one hour, longer if possible, as coarse oatmeal requires a lot of cooking, stirring occasionally to prevent burning.

Rolled oats take about half an hour to cook.

Dry Hash

For each person, allow ½ lb of potatoes, 4 oz salt, fresh or tinned meat, 1 small onion, pepper, salt, and a little mixed herbs. Cook the potatoes and mash them, chop the meat and onion fine, and add to the potatoes; season and mix well. Put into a greased dish, smooth the top, and ornament with a knife. Bake in the oven until brown on the top. Serve hot. If you have no oven, make a piece of iron hot, and brown the top with that.

Irish Stew

Allow for each person 6 oz of neck or breast of mutton, 6 oz potatoes, 1 onion, pepper and salt. Chop up the meat into 2-inch pieces; put into a saucepan, nearly cover with hot water, bring to the boil and skim, add pepper and salt. Simmer for half an hour. Add vegetables and finish cooking for another three quarters of an hour. If procurable, turnips may be used.

Hot Pot

Allow for each person 6 oz of fresh meat, ½ lb potatoes, 1 onion, pepper, salt and a little mixed herbs. Cut up the meat into pieces, roll them in flour and put them into a pie-dish or tin dish. Cut up the onion and sprinkle over the meat, also the seasoning. Nearly cover with stock or water. Cut the potatoes up, and arrange on the top. Bake 1 ¼ hours. This can be made in two or three tiers in a deep dish.

Haricot Mutton

Allow 6 oz of neck of mutton, 1 onion, 1 carrot, 1 turnip, a tablespoon of flour, pepper, salt and water. Cut up the mutton, peel the onion, turnip and carrot; cut them into slices. Put a little clean dripping into a stewpan; when hot and a blue smoke rises, brown a few pieces of meat at a time; when brown, take out and keep hot. Then brown the onion, add the flour and slightly brown. Add stock or water sufficient to nearly cover the meat. Add the seasoning, put in the meat and vegetables, and simmer 1 ¼ hours. Skim off the fat and serve. Put the meat on a hot dish, place the vegetables on the top, pour over the gravy.

Stewed Steak

Proceed the same as for Haricot Mutton, omitting the turnip.

Meat Pie

Allow 6 oz of cooked meat, or preserved, to each person, 1 small onion, pepper, salt, flour and herbs. Cut up the meat, put into a pie dish; cut up the onion and put in; season with pepper, salt, herbs, and a little flour. Pour over this enough water to nearly fill the dish.

Paste to cover the pie: 4 oz of flour, ¼ teaspoonful of baking powder, small pinch of salt, 2 oz dripping. Rub in the dripping, mix up with a little water, roll out, wet the edge of the dish, put a boarder round, wet the border with water, place on the top paste, cut round the dish with a sharp knife, notch the edge, prick a hole in the top, make some leaves with the paste left over, put on top and bake for 40 minutes (about).

Cottage Pie

Peel and boil some potatoes. When done, mash them with a little dripping, pepper and salt. Grease a pie dish or tin; line with mashed potatoes; chop an onion and some cooked meat very fine, add a little flour, pepper, salt and mixed herbs; moisten with a little stock or water, fill up the dish, put the rest of the potatoes on top, smooth with a knife and bake a golden brown (about half an hour).

Baked Meat

See the oven is hot by placing a pinch of flour on the middle shelf; close the oven door for 1 minute. If it is a golden brown it is about 380 degrees of heat; if black, too hot; not coloured, not hot enough. This test is good for baking anything.

Cut the joints into pieces from 4 to 8 lbs. Allow 15 minutes for thin pieces of beef or mutton, and 15 minutes over; thick pieces, 20 minutes to the lb. and 20 minutes over; veal and pork, 20 minutes and 25 minutes, according to thickness.

The meat should be put on a rest, and put in a double tin, with water between. Baste the meat well with dripping, and turn over once or twice. When done, turn the dripping into a basin or jar, put a little water in the tin, a little salt, heat over the fire, and pour round the meat – not over.

Boiled Meat

Allow same time for boiled as for baked meat. Put into boiling water. If the liquor is required for soup, put the meat into hot water.

Stewed Rabbit

1 rabbit, ½ lb salt pork or bacon, 1 onion, 2 oz rice, 1 teaspoon mixed herbs, some pepper, salt and water.

Skin, clean, and wash the rabbit; cut into joints and place in salted water for ½ hour. Put into enough boiling water to cover it; bring to a boil and skim. Peel and cut up the onion, add to the rabbit, with the bacon cut up, pepper, salt, herbs and rice. Cook for 1½ hours. If required thick, mix a little flour with cold water, and thicken. Serve on a hot dish.

Bowline Hash

Take some potatoes, cooked meat, onion, pepper, salt and flour. Cut up the onion, cut up meat and potatoes into small square dice. Put a little dripping into a saucepan and brown the onion. Add a little flour and brown slightly; put in sufficient water to make the quantity of gravy required, season with pepper and salt, simmer for about 15 minutes, strain and add the potatoes to the gravy, and cook. When done, put in the meat and warm thoroughly. Cooked meat should not be boiled a second time, as it makes it tough. Serve hot.

Sea Pie (for 16 persons)

4 lbs fresh meat, 4 lbs potatoes, 1 lb onions, 2 quarts water, some pepper and salt.

For the paste: 2 lbs flour, 2 teaspoonfuls of baking powder, ¾ lb dripping or suet, some salt and water.

Method for Sea Pie: Wash and peel the potatoes; do not cut them. Peel and slice the onion; cut the meat into 2-inch pieces. Put the water in a saucepan, season with pepper and salt, and bring to the boil. Add a little salt and the baking powder to the flour, and mix well; lightly rub in the fat, and take sufficient water to make into a medium dough. Divide into two pieces. Put one-half of the meat into the boiling water, half of the onions, and half of the potatoes. Roll out one piece of dough the size of the saucepan lid, and lay this on the top to form the first deck. Put in the remaining portion of the meat, onions and potatoes, and roll out the second deck and lay on top, cutting a hole in the centre. Simmer gently for two hours. When done, cut the top deck into four and remove, take out the first layer of meat and potatoes and put on a dish; cut the lower deck into four and remove, put the remaining meat and potatoes on a dish, skim off the fat, pour the liquor over the meat, put the pieces of paste on top to serve.

Savoury Goose (for 6 persons)

1 lb potatoes, ½ lb bacon or salt pork, 2 oz flour, 1 teaspoonful of sage and onion, 1 lb liver, salt, pepper, and water to cover.

Peel and partly cook the potatoes. Cut the liver and bacon into slices, also cut the potatoes into slices and the onions into rings. Dip the liver into flour, and put a layer in the bottom of the pie dish; sprinkle a little sage over and pepper; then a layer of onion rings, layer of bacon, layer of potatoes; repeat until dish is full; mix rest of flour with water, and pour over.

Bake for 1 ¼ hours. Should the dish get dry in cooking, add a little water; should potatoes be highly coloured, remove them before serving.

Bone Stock

Take some bones and chop or crack them up; put into cold water, bring to a boil and skim well. Add a little onion, carrot, turnip cut up, 2 or 3 cloves procurable. If you want a brown stock, brown the onions in a little fat before adding to the stock.

Savoury Omelettes

Break eggs into a basin; add pepper, salt and a little mixed herbs; put a little clean dripping or butter in a frying pan, make hot, beat up eggs, put in pan, stir round with fork until it just begins to set, then shape into a cushion or pillar, shape at the side of the pan. When nearly brown on the bottom side, turn over on a hot dish, sprinkle a little chopped parsley on the top, and serve hot. This should never be made until it is wanted.

Plum Duff

1lb. flour, 1 teaspoonful baking powder, 4 oz fat or chopped suet, pinch of salt, 6 oz raisins, 4 oz brown sugar and some water.

Sift flour, baking powder and salt; rub in dripping and add suet; stone plums and add sugar; mix all together with sufficient water. Put dough into duff bags, or steam in bouilli tins. Boil for 4 hours or steam for 5 hours. When serving, cut each man's portion. If allowed, serve sweet sauce with this pudding. This is two men's allowance.

Rice Pudding (with eggs)

½ lb rice, 4 oz sugar, 1 pint milk, 2 eggs, and some nutmeg.

Wash the rice well and boil in plenty of water, strain off and pour into a pie dish. Make a custard with the eggs, milk and sugar, and stir into the rice. Grate a little nutmeg on top. Bake until well set and serve.

Rice Pudding (no eggs)

½ lb rice, 4 oz sugar, 2 oz finely chopped suet, 2 tablespoonfuls custard powder and 1 pint milk or water.

Wash and boil rice with sugar and suet. When done, mix custard powder with a little cold water, and stir in. Put into a greased pie dish and bake a golden brown on top.

Rice Pudding (another way)

Wash 4 oz of rice, put into a pie dish, pour over a pint of cold milk, add 2 oz sugar, put into oven until cooked. If it gets dry, add a little more milk as it is baking. Serve with castor sugar over it.

Flapjacks

1 lb flour, 1 teaspoonful baking powder, small pinch salt, 4 oz currants, grate of nutmeg and some milk or water.

Wash, clean and dry currants, sift flour and mix all together to make a moderate soft batter. Heat some fat in a shallow frying pan, drop in a tablespoonful at a time, and fry both sides brown. Drain and dust with castor sugar.

Plain Scones

1 lb flour, 1 teaspoonful baking powder and pinch of salt.

Sift flour, baking powder and salt together; rub in 3 oz butter, mix to a dough with milk. Roll out about ½ inch thick, cut into wedge pieces, 16 to the lb. Place on a baking sheet, prick over with a fork, wash over with milk and bake about 20 minutes. When ready, cut open and butter.

Damper

1 lb flour, a little salt, teaspoonful of bicarbonate of soda, 3 oz clean fat or butter and a little sour milk or buttermilk.

Mix flour, salt and soda together; rub in the fat, mix with the milk in a dough, break into 4 pieces, roll them round, put on a hot baking sheet and bake each side on top of the stove. Proper damper is baked on hot stones in a hole dug in the earth.

Baking Powder Rolls

Take 1 lb flour, sifted, with a little suet and a heaped-up teaspoonful baking powder. Rub in 3 oz butter, mix into a dough with milk, break into 16 pieces, make into different rolls, crescents, cottages, twists, knots and horseshoes. Put on a baking sheet, bake 20 minutes. You must be very quick over this, because of the baking powder.

[All the recipes given in this chapter are simple and thoroughly practical for camp cooking, either in ordinary stoves or camp stoves or oven.]

Sauces

Melted Butter

1 oz butter; 1½ oz flour, water. Melt butter in a saucepan, add flour and work it well together with a wooden spoon; add sufficient boiling gradually, and make it into a smooth sauce the thickness of cream – do not have it lumpy. This sauce is the foundation for a good many sauces. Add sugar and lime juice – you have a sweet sauce; a little chopped parsley, pepper, and salt – parsley sauce; a teaspoonful of anchovy essence – anchovy sauce; a few capers and a little vinegar – caper sauce; and several other sauces can be made.

Marmalade, Jam or Syrup Sauce

Put ½ pint water into a saucepan, add 2 oz sugar, 2 tablespoonfuls of marmalade, jam or syrup. Mix a teaspoonful of cornflour in a little water. When the other boils, thicken with the cornflour, and cook for 5 minutes. These sauces are used for different boiled puddings.

Cleaning

When scrubbing white boards or tables, do not use soda – use a little soap, a little sand and plenty of water. Soda makes the boards look yellow, instead of white.

Scouring Mess Kidds and Tin Utensils

Do not use sand or brick dust, use Monkey Brand soap or a little Pynka mixed with ammonia. If none of these are procurable, get some fine clay and damp with water; rub the tin with this – it will not scratch; then wash well, dry well and polish with dry flour. This not only polishes, but prevents the tins from getting rusty. If, when you are washing the tins, you put a little soft soap and soda in the hot water, wash the tins and dry well while hot, and polish with flour; they will keep clear for a week.

Cleaning Knives

If very much stained, cut a potato in half and rub the knife. Then, if you have no board, take a piece of canvas, rub some brick dust on it, fold it in two, and pull the knife in and out towards you, then dust them.

To Clean Silver or White Metal

Clean silver with whitening mixed with water, then wash in very hot water with a little soda and soft soap; take out and dry them while they are quite hot. It will give them a fine polish.

To clean saucepans, frying pans or baking pans when discoloured, rub them well with dry salt and silver sand.

General

Mix mustard with hot water; it keeps longer than with cold.

If, when seasoning a dish, it is too salt, mix a little sugar and vinegar together, and add a little to the dish. It will counteract the salt, and, vice versa, if too sweet, add a little salt.

If you have no paste board, use a piece of canvas.

If you have no rolling pin, use a bottle, it is very cool.

If you think the water is tainted, boil it with a few drops of lemon juice; it will sweeten it.

CYCLIST BADGE

> A Scout must sign a certificate that he owns a bicycle in good working order, which he is willing to use in the King's service if called upon at any time in case of emergency.

Now as to the various requirements for getting the badge.

A Cyclist Scout must own a Bicycle in Good Working Order: The words "in good working order" mean that your cycle must always be ready for use, the tyres must be in fairly good condition, you must have at least one brake in thorough working order, must possess a proper lamp and bell, and must carry a complete repair-outfit and set of spanners with you.

A Cyclist Scout must be able to ride his Bicycle satisfactorily: That is, you must be able to ride on level ground at the rate of, at least eight miles per hour, and you should be able to ride up ordinary small hills without dismounting. In addition, you will find it of great assistance to be able to mount and dismount by the back step, and by either pedal. You should also be able to turn round either by the right or by the left.

A Cyclist Scout must be able to read a Map: The map referred to is an ordinary road map or cycle map.

A Cyclist Scout must be able to repeat correctly a Verbal Message: If you have not got a good memory (and this is a thing which all Scouts should have), you must train it. One of the ways in which you can do this, is to get a member of your Patrol to give you a short message; do not write it down, but, about an hour afterwards, see if you can repeat it correctly to him. Continue this practice, gradually increasing the length of the message and the time between receiving and delivering it, until you can eventually repeat a long message correctly 24 hours after you receive it.

When a Cyclist Scout is given a verbal message to deliver, before starting he should repeat it and be perfectly certain that he understands every word of it.

If given a written message, he should read it over carefully and see that he understands it, then learn it by heart in case he should have to destroy it. He must never alter anything in a message. If he thinks there is a mistake, or that the message would be made more intelligible by adding a few words, he should point it out to the sender and ask him to alter it should he consider it advisable.

Before starting, a Cyclist Scout should also ask the following questions:

If he is to bring a reply and where it is to be brought to?

What he is to do if the person to whom the message is addressed is not found at the place indicated in the message?

Where he is to report himself after delivering the message.

A Cyclist Scout must be able to repair Punctures etc. It is unnecessary to detail here how to mend a puncture, but the following few hints may be of use to you.

If you require to mend a puncture on a country road, and find you have no tyre lever, cut off a bit from the branch of a tree, about 6 or 8 inches long, and an inch to an inch-and-a-half in diameter; make one end like the blade of a knife for

$2^1/2$ inches, and you have a tyre-lever ready made.

Always put nuts, screws and valves into a place of safety; the best place is your trouser pocket.

A good way to keep a patch in position until the solution is dry, is to place one penny above the patch and another penny at the other side of the tyre beneath the patch, and either place a weight on top, or keep the coins together with a trouser clip.

Keep your cycle well oiled (not forgetting the pedals); very few people oil their bicycles nearly enough.

Before going out for a run, try all your nuts with your spanner, see your oil can is full, also your lamp, try your brake to see if it is in good order, and be sure you have spanners and a repair outfit – not forgetting valve rubber.

Finally, remember that on ceasing to own a bicycle you must return your badge to your Scoutmaster.

ELECTRICIAN BADGE

A Scout must have a knowledge of method of rescue and resuscitation of a person insensible from shock.

Be able to make a simple electromagnet; have elementary knowledge of action of simple battery cells and know the working of electric bells and telephones.

Understand and be able to remedy fused wire, and to repair broken electric connections.

We have all heard the story rumoured to the late Lord Kelvin, who, when going the round of a large electrical work, asked one of the men, "What is electricity?" The man, confused, said that he "didn't know". Whereupon, Lord Kelvin replied, "Neither do I." Well, we may take Lord Kelvin here to mean that there is more in the subject than has been discovered, and that whatever it is capable of, and whatever term it is known by, it is an element of the universe like unto water, air etc., inasmuch as no one can make it or destroy it. All the dynamos, batteries and frictional machines in the world couldn't make enough electricity to make a fly wink. These appliances only collect it either by friction or by chemical action.

We have all tried to magnetize a piece of amber by rubbing and many of us have thought amber was the only thing capable of this action, but let us try a piece of glass and we shall see that the same result can be obtained.

Before the dawn of the Christian era, 2000 years ago, amber was known to have the property mentioned, but it was not until the seventeenth century that one of Queen Elizabeth's doctors discovered that it was quite a common property of matter. This doctor, although he proved that that phenomenon was common to all substances, called it after amber, as this was the substance which had been known to have an attractive property for so many centuries. The Greek word for amber being "elektron", it is said that the term electricity was immediately assumed; and, when a body was "excited" or rubbed, and exhibited this attractive property, it was said to be "electrified".

The reader, then, will understand that electricity is not made but collected – or generated, as it is more generally termed.

To begin, we will take the tests in their order as written in the book.

Rescue

It must be clearly understood that some care is necessary in attempting rescue. When a person is unfortunate enough to touch any naked conductor carrying current of sufficient pressure, he receives an unpleasant reminder.

The cause of this is, that the nerves and muscles are drawn taut as with a jerk. In attempting rescue, we should have a knowledge of the dangers, just as a man should be a swimmer before he attempts a rescue from drowning.

Well, we must know what articles and materials are conductors of electricity. For this it is only necessary to know what articles are conductors and nonconductors, that we are likely to come across in a case of that kind.

Conductors
Metals of any kind.

Stone or concrete (which is always damp, more or less).

Water or liquids.

Damp wood.

Anything which has damp about it.

Nonconductors
Rubber.

Gutta-percha.

Wood which is thoroughly dry.

Glass.

Mackintosh waterproofs.

Cloth which is dry.

High-pressure currents will travel through clothes by the natural perspiration from the body.

Now, should it be uncertain whether an injured person is free from current, it is best to procure something by which to handle him or something on which to stand, of such a nature that the current cannot find a way through by way of your own body to the earth or ground. If rubber gloves are available, these should be slipped on at once as no time should be lost. A dry mackintosh or box, or a sheet of rubber or glass is necessary even in the case of low-pressure currents, say below 250 volts.

In the case of very high pressure, it is necessary to be even more careful, as wood is only a very poor insulator in the high pressures, say from 500 to 10,000 volts. A hole in a rubber glove at the finger-ends is likely to be very disastrous in the case of handling 5,000 volts, as the perspiration from the hand, however slight, would coat the inside of the hole and provide a path for the current into the body.

Resuscitation

Having cleared our patient from all further danger, it is now necessary to bring him back to consciousness and well-being. To do this, most medical men recommend Sylvester's Method of Artificial Respiration as being the best.

Death may be caused by electric shock in two different ways, viz.:

By shock to the nerve centres, thereby causing a naturally weak heart to cease beating.

By shock to the nerves, causing the muscles to contract, and the tongue to be drawn into the throat, where it would probably lodge and suffocate an insensible person; thus, shock contracting the muscles or tongue causes asphyxia.

In the latter case, the tongue should be gripped and pulled out, and then tied down with a hankerchief under the chin to prevent it slipping back.

Be able to make a simple electromagnet

Everybody has seen an electromagnet in some form or other, but perhaps they don't know how to recognize it when they do see one. Did you ever see an electricbell without an electromagnet? No!

There are very many different uses for electro-magnets, some of which are electric-bells, relays, motors (electric), crane lifters, magnets for sorting out steel or iron from other material, railway signals etc.

The chief points of electromagnets are: The magnet is only a magnet while the current is travelling through the winding, and ceases to pull or to exert any attraction when the current is off. We can, therefore, cause a movement many miles away without any mechanical transmission of energy or power.

It is even possible to unlock a door from a distance by means of electric control, or to release a weight, for which many people find a use.

Elementary knowledge of the working of electric-bells and telephones

We don't propose to attempt here to go very deeply into the intricacies of telephone-work, as we not that in the test "elementary" is the word used. We cannot begin this portion better than by giving a diagram of an electric-bell circuit.

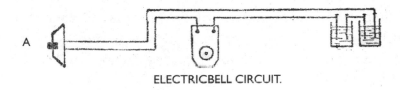

ELECTRICBELL CIRCUIT.

We shall see above that the push A is normally a break in the circuit, which, when it is pressed, causes the circuit to be made complete, and allows the battery to generate current, thus the bell to come into action. The current flows from the terminal of the porous pot through the bell, and back to the zinc.

The push is a contrivance having two contacts which, when not in use, are kept apart by a spring. These two contacts are each connected by an insulated wire to battery and bell respectively. Thus, when we depress with the thumb, the two contacts are connected together, allowing the wires (which are normally separate) to form a path through which the current can travel.

The bell is an instrument which is formed of an electro-magnet, an armature attached to a spring, a contact pillar, a base-board and cover, two terminals, a hammer and a gong.

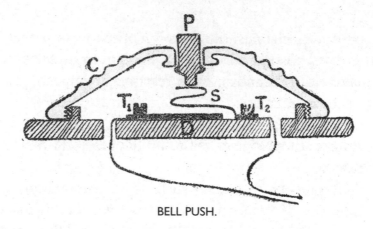

BELL PUSH.

The action of the bell is such that when the push button is depressed, a current flows along the wires through the winding of the electromagnet, by the terminal, to the frame, which is metal. Through the frame it travels, and along the spring on the armature, to the contact pillar, and out by the

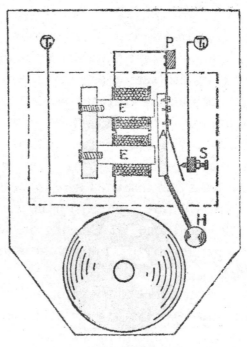

ELECTRIC BELL.

terminal. On pressing the button, it will be seen that the action of the magnet would be to draw the armature towards its poles and break contact between the contact pillar, and the spring. Then the current being cut off, the magnet releases its draw on the armature, and the spring flies back to its normal position, touching the contact pillar only to allow a current to flow and repeat the described action, which happens several hundred times per minute, thus a trembling sound is heard on the gong.

Telephones

Most people are nowadays quite used to these necessary instruments, and we think that a little explanation of the "whys and wherefores" is all that is necessary for our purpose, because, were we to attempt to enter into the intricate technicalities of telephones, we should need many pages of introduction to a subject which is almost worthy of being called a distinct profession.

Well, the ordinary simple telephone, used for speaking from one place to another, will be quite enough for our purpose. It consists mainly of a transmitter, receiver, a bell for calling up, and a battery for ringing and speaking.

ENGINEER BADGE

A Scout must have a general idea of the working of motorcars and
steam locomotives, marine, internal combustion, and electric
engines.

He must know the names of the principal parts and their functions;
how to start, drive, feed, stop and lubricate any one of them chosen by
himself.

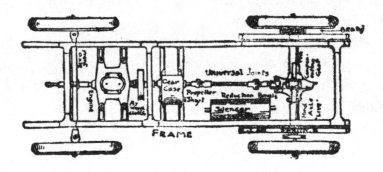

FRAME OF A MOTOR CAR

ENTERTAINER BADGE

A Scout must be able to entertain by himself a mixed audience for at least 15 minutes with a varied programme from the following: Recitations, songs, playing banjo, penny whistle and mouth organ, conjuring tricks, character sketches, stories, ventriloquism, stump speeches and step-dancing.

SCOUTS PERFORMING SONGS, RECITATIONS
AND SMALL PLAYS AROUND THE CAMP FIRE.
From an original drawing by Robert Baden-Powell.

FARMER BADGE

A Scout must have a knowledge gained by practice of ploughing, cultivating, drilling, hedging, and draining. He must also have a working knowledge of farm machinery, haymaking, reaping, leading and stacking and a general acquaintance with the routine seasonal work on a farm, including the care of cattle, horses, sheep and pigs.

Before dealing with the individual operations on a farm, it may be advisable to say something about the general principles of farm management, in order to give the reader an idea of rotations etc. The system of cropping varies in different districts and with different methods of farming, but a very common one in Scotland is – first year, lea oats; second year, turnips, mangold or potatoes; third year, sown-out oats; forth year, hay or pasture; then pasture for one or several years.

Autumn ploughing: It will now be best to describe the routine work, and in doing this to begin immediately after harvest. After the stacks are neatly thatched, and everything tidied up, autumn ploughing is commenced on the lea stubble, i.e. land which has just borne its first crop of oats and which is to be prepared for turnips. This is ploughed first so that the soil may be acted upon by the frost and air, which have a very beneficial effect in loosening it and making it easier to work in Spring. Two horses are used for ploughing. The plough is a comparatively simple implement, but it occasionally needs repair to the wearing parts.

Meantime, other occupations are being carried out on the farm. The potatoes are being lifted, and the turnips are being cleared and stored in pits for winter use.

Frost will probably come in November, and, as no ploughing can be done then, the carting and spreading of accumulated farmyard manure may be proceeded with; the hardness of the ground makes an easy draft for horses, and prevents the cutting up the fields. It is often put on the sown-out land, i.e. land which is being laid down in pasture, and sometimes on grass land. All through the winter the corn has to be thrashed and the straw made into bundles.

It is now about the end of March, at which time the corn is sown. This is either done by the drill or by hand, both methods being quite satisfactory, though sowing by the drilling machine takes longer. A man when sowing has a sheetful of corn strapped round his shoulders, and he dips his hand in alternately, and scatters the corn by a semi-circular swing of the arms. Care should be taken not to miss any land, and the best safeguard against this is to do the work systematically. At the same time, a man is harrowing in the seed with a pair of horses and harrows; he first harrows the way the furrows run, then from corner to corner, then he goes across the furrows from side to side. Attention is next turned to the fallow, or turnip ground, which is first gone over either with a grubber or a cultivator; the former is heavier and goes deeper, but both implements are wrought by three horses. The ground is next harrowed and the weeds gathered off, and by this time the soil is in a well-cultivated state. Drilling is then commenced; the drill is just like a plough, but there are mouldboards on both sides, and the ground is turned over equally to right and left.

Manure is then sown in these drills and the plough is entered in the middle of the piled-up soil, which is turned over again on to the manure, which is thus immediately below where the turnips are sown. The seed is then sown by the turnip barrow, which sows two drills at a time, and the field is left till hoeing time comes.

It is now June and time to cut the hay. This is done with a two-horse reaper, and the swathes are left for a day in the sun, till they are well dried on top, then they are turned over by a horse tedder, a swaths turner or hay-rakes. The reaper cuts 4- to 5-feet swathes and can cut about 8 acres a day. When the hay is dry and brown, it is raked into rows, from which it is swept into heaps by the horse sweep, and built into ricks, which contain about a cartload of hay.

About the beginning of September, harvest commences, and this is the busiest and most anxious time on a farm, because there is so much at stake. Cutting should be commenced when the oats are uniformly tinged with yellow; openings are made with the scythe round the edges of the field, to give the self-binder work room. This wonderful piece of machinery is drawn by three horses; as the corn is cut, it falls on to a revolving canvas, on which it is conveyed to the foot of the frame, where it is received between two other canvases, and carried up to the buncher, where it is divided into sheaves, tied, and thrown out. This machine needs a capable man to work it, as the mechanism sometimes goes wrong, and if not speedily put right much time is lost.

Cattle which are being wintered outside should get from 2 to 4 lbs cotton or soya cake, with a liberal allowance of hay or straw, and some turnips; but, in the summer time, on good land, young cattle do well without any concentrated feeding. Of course, if cattle are being fattened, they should have a liberal allowance of cake, even on good pasture.

Horses on hard work should be well fed and cared for; they should be thoroughly brushed, and their stalls cleaned both morning and evening.

Sheep are hardy animals, if properly cared for. They must be dipped at least twice a year, and when a sheep shows signs of lameness it should be at once caught and its feet pared, for a lame sheep never fattens well. When sheep are being fattened, it is a common practice to "fold" them on turnips, i.e. to surround them with bars and to cut the turnips for them, although they are sometimes made to eat the turnips growing, but this involves considerable waste.

Pigs are useful at a farm for eating what would otherwise be wasted: coarse porridge, old potatoes, green stalks, whey etc., are all given, so a pig can be fattened more cheaply than any other animal. They should always be kept clean and warm, and get plenty of exercise, otherwise their legs are apt to go wrong.

Hedges should be cut every year, and in most leases the tenant is bound to do so. It is generally done in the slack times, in frosty weather, or between haytime and harvest.

FIREMAN BADGE

A Scout must know:

How to give the alarm to inhabitants, police etc.

How to enter burning buildings. How to prevent spread of fire.

The use of hose, unrolling, joining up, hydrants, use of nozzles, etc.

The use of escape ladders and shutes; improvising ropes, jumping sheets etc.

The fireman's lift, how to drag a patient, how to work in fumes etc.

The use of fire extinguishers.

How to rescue animals.

How to save property, climb and pass buckets.

"Scrum" to keep back crowd.

The first thing to do in the case of fire, is to warn the inhabitants of the house.

Either go or send someone to break the nearest fire alarm.

It is as well to note that after having rung the alarm, it is necessary to wait till the fire brigade arrives, in order to direct them to where the fire is.

Tell the policeman on the beat.

After the arrival of the fire brigade, there is little to be done, as the firemen, who are trained to the work, will probably be present in sufficient strength to do all that is required.

A Scout, however, if he gets the opportunity, should offer his services to the firemaster in charge for messages, etc. But nothing should be done without an order given by the firemaster.

In places where there are no fire brigades, or where it takes a brigade some time to reach the fire, much can be done by a properly organised patrol of Scouts.

The following is a memorandum by Captain Wells, the Headquarters' Commissioner for firework. Captain Wells was Chief of the London Fire Brigade, and was asked by Headquarters to draft a memorandum for guidance in qualifying for the Fireman's Badge. Basis on which fire examination in fire brigade work should be conducted:

1. Candidates must have a good knowledge of the locality, especially with regard to population, roads, buildings, factories, water supply in case of fire, telegraph offices, telephone facilities (principally geographical knowledge is required).

2. Should have qualified in first aid and ambulance work.

3. Should have attended twenty drills in fire-brigade work, and be proficient in rope knots, slinging and lowering a human being (knowledge only of chair knot or equivalent).

4. Experience in jumping from a height of 10 feet into a net or sheet.

5. Fireman's lift carrying a boy his own size down and up, twelve steps, or thirty yards on level.

6. (Telegraph form.) Write a descriptive message of a fire in twenty-four words. Should be able to use a bicycle or ride a horse.

7. General knowledge of simple fire brigade apparatus, rope work, ladder, hand pump, jumping sheet etc. Some knowledge of patent extinguisher likely to be met with in buildings.

Note. A nervous boy, or one not sound in heart or lungs, should not be encouraged to take part in this work.

FRIEND TO ANIMALS BADGE

A Scout must have a general knowledge of the anatomy of domestic and farm animals, and be able to describe treatment and symptoms of the following: wounds, fractures and sprains, exhaustion, choking, lameness. He must understand shoeing and shoes; and must be able to give a drench for colic.

Wounds

Preliminary Steps: The first step in all wounds is to arrest excessive haemorrhage; the second to cleanse the wound and apply a dressing.

1. Arresting Haemorrhage: Haemorrhage will either be from an artery or from a vein. If from a large artery, the blood will be pumped out in jerks, and from any artery it is always of a bright colour. Haemorrhage can as a rule be arrested by direct pressure, but if this does not suffice, no time must be lost in endeavouring to compress the artery somewhere between the wound and the heart.

2. Cleansing and Dressing the Wound: When the haemorrhage has been stopped, the wound should be cleansed with a weak antiseptic solution, such as perchloride of mercury solution (one tabloid to a pint of water) or a solution of Jeyes' Fluid, phenyle, or permanganate of potash, all foreign substances being removed. The dressing should then be put on, and if the situation of the wound admits, a bandage should be applied over a wad of tow soaked in the dressing.

Fractures

Fractures which it is possible to treat, and Method of Treatment: Bone unites with horses just as readily as with other animals, but the difficulty is to maintain the complete apposition of the bones which is necessary to ensure perfect repair, and, unless recovery is absolute, horses are useless for general purposes. It is rarely considered advisable, for instance, to attempt treatment in the case of fracture of the long bones of the limbs, and it is certainly not worthwhile where a joint is involved. On the other hand, many fractures do very well, such as some fractures of the pelvis, face and jaws, etc., and split pasterns. In the absence of skilled advice, it is often difficult to decide whether fractures exist or not. If a horse can put any weight on a limb, it is wise to give it the benefit of the doubt and not destroy it. Pending the arrival of skilled aid nothing can very well be done.

Lameness and Sprains

Lameness: This is a difficult subject, requiring special knowledge and experience. The cause is often not at all apparent even to a qualified observer. The following are some of the most obvious causes of lameness: contusions from brushing, overreaching, sprains, foot injuries, such as corns, bruising of the sole, or a nail which has been picked up, or thrush. Where the cause is not apparent, it is always wise to remove the shoe and search the foot. If any of these causes are found, they should be treated accordingly.

Sprains: In almost all cases of lameness rest from work is necessary. This is particularly the case with sprains. Sprain of muscle is rapidly and completely repaired, because muscles are plentifully supplied with blood vessels, but lowly organised structures like tendons and ligaments take longer to repair, and recovery is less complete.

Diseases – General Treatment

Nursing: The importance of providing the best conditions for sick horses cannot be exaggerated. The chief considerations are fresh air, shelter, shade from the sun, if necessary light, warm clothing, a good bed to lie upon, light, digestible food, hand-rubbing and light bandaging of the legs, and frequent changes of position when weak and unable to rise.

Method of giving a Draught: A draught may be given to a horse by means of a wine bottle, preferably a hock or champagne bottle. The horse's head should be raised by means of a soft rope loop attached to a broom or fork, or twitch (see below). The lower jaw should be free, as this assists the act of swallowing. The person giving the draught should insert the neck of the bottle inside the cheek and pour out until the mouth is full. Time should be given for the horse to swallow, and then more given, and so on.

Colic: Colic is often associated with fatigue. A horse that is tired and that is in the reaction stage after fatigue, cannot digest food in any quantity, and colic is often the result. In the absence of skilled advice, it is best to assume in every case of colic that there is obstruction of the bowels. This is relieved by a quickly acting purgative of sufficient strength. For this purpose nothing is so good as an ordinary "physic" (aloes) ball dissolved in a little hot water and made up to a pint with cold water. For an ordinary-sized horse, 5 drachms is sufficient; for a large horse, 6 drachms; for a pong, 4 drachms. The giving of opiates should not be resorted to except when the pain is persistent. A stimulant may always be given with advantage. As a last resource, one ounce of laudanum may be given to relieve the pain until the action of the draught is established.

Debility: Debility may be due to a variety of causes. It is safe to state that horses in this condition should be excused from work altogether if this course is possible. Liberty to graze, and the gentle exercise thus afforded, will be all in their favour.

Exhaustion: Horses apparently incapable of going a step further may be got home by giving them stimulants in small quantities, frequently repeated, and by giving them time to recover and assisting their movements. Cases all but hopeless may be revived by strychnine given hypodermically, but, needless to say, such cases require professional treatment.

Shoeing and Shoes

To understand shoeing and shoes, a Scout must first understand the construction of a horse's foot.

The object of shoeing is to protect the foot and give a natural foothold. The shoe should be made to fit the horse's foot, and the horn not cut and carved to fit the shoe. Therefore, handmade shoes are much to be preferred to machine-made ones.

In preparing the hoof for the shoe, don't touch the sole or frog. The wall should be rasped down until level with the sole where it joins the wall. Never rasp the outside of the wall, as this takes away the natural outer varnish and thus weakens the horn. Place the hot shoe on the foot, and see that it is level from toe to heel. If it is not, take it off and remedy any defects. Do not let the shoe fit itself on by burning the horn.

SURFACE OF THE FOOT

a – Point of frog.
b – Cleft of frog.
d – Sole.
e – Wall
f – White line dividing wall and sole.
gg – Bars formed by the folding inwards of the wall at the heels.

A well shod foot.   A foot badly shod and spoilt by shortening or dumpling.

GARDENER BADGE

A Scout must dig a piece of ground not less than 12 feet square.
Know the names of a dozen plants pointed out in an ordinary garden.
Understand what is meant by pruning, grafting and manuring.
Plant and grow successfully six kinds of vegetables or flowers from
seeds or cuttings.

WORKING HARD FOR THE GARDENER BADGE

HANDYMAN BADGE

A Scout must be able to paint a door or bath, whitewash a ceiling, repair gas-fittings, tap washes, sash lines, window and door fastenings, replace gas mantles and electriclight bulbs, hang pictures and curtains, repair blinds, fix curtains and portiere rods, blind fixtures, lay carpets, mend clothing and upholstery, do small furniture and china repairs, and sharpen knives.

As an alternative to repairing gasfittings and the replacing of gas mantles and electric light bulbs, he must be able to put glass in windows, prepare and hang papers on walls, and repair cane-bottom chairs.

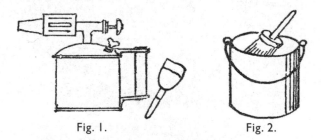

Fig. I.   Fig. 2.

Paint a door or bath

After making a choice of colour, obtain a large sash tool or pound brush (these brushes being handiest for jobs that have a fairly large plain area) and a lump of pumice stone to clean the old paint off, if it has been previously painted. The tradesman, of course, would use his blowlamp and scraper (Fig.1.) in the case of a door. When a good "ground" has been obtained, take a small quantity of paint on the brush, which should not be dipped more than halfway in, and even then have most of the paint adhering patted of onto the tin side (Fig. 2.). Work this well into the object, making the strokes up and down or from left to right and back again, not in circles or crisscross. Repeat this until all the surface is evenly coated. Let this dry, clean up with rough glasspaper or pumice, used lightly, and repeat.

There is a special bath enamel sold by oilmen, which is far better for this work, as ordinary paint is inclined to get sticky if very hot water is used.

Whitewashing

Whitewash can be made from quick-lime or whiting. It is made from quicklime by "slacking"; that is to say, the quantity of lime required is put into a bucket or tub, and a small quantity of water poured over it, when it will crumble into powder. This is then mixed with more water into a thick cream consistency, which is further reduced as required, by adding more water. Whiting is simply mixed with water to a nice full consistency, not watery or heavy. Powdered blue is then added in both cases, until there is the faintest blue tint; this gives a much better white when dry.

Fig. 3.

The limewash is preferable in situations which are in any way inclined to harbour germs.

There are also many patent distempers sold, directions for mixing being given on the packages.

Now take your brush, which should be of a broad, flat design (Fig. 3.), dip and pat off on the side of the bucket any superfluous whitewash, then apply to the wall or ceiling with long straight strokes.

When working on ceilings it is as well to make a small scaffold by putting a plank across two pairs of steps (Fig. 4.). If a brush with a long handle is used, don't forget the "drip-ring" (Fig. 5.), or at least a piece of cloth tied round the handle about a yard from the head of the brush.

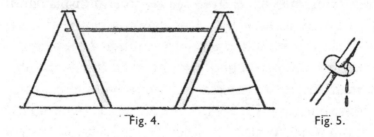

Fig. 4.   Fig. 5.

Repairs to Gas Fittings, and Fixing Mantles

The fittings are those parts of the brackets or pendants which are not soldered to the lead supply pipe (Fig. 6.). The authorities usually demand that all connections with the supply pipes be made by a registered plumber.

The common faults are leakage at the joints, or burst or worn-out tubes. Leakage can often be remedied by tightening up the parts by screwing. If this is not successful, remove the screw and daub the thread of the screw with white of red lead and then screw up again. Don't put any lead inside the pipe or

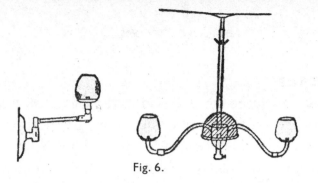

Fig. 6.

elbow, as this would likely stop up the burner.

Tap Washers are fixed to the lower end of the spindle, which is turned upper butterfly or capstan end. When the tap is shut, the washer is pressed firmly onto the seat of the valve and keeps the water from passing. When time and wear have made the washer hard and uneven the tap drips. To renew the washer, turn water off at the main (if this is not done, there is every probability of a splendid fountain display and a rather wet handyman), and, with a spanner, unscrew the nut immediately beneath the movable portion (Fig. 11.). The whole of the top will now lift off and expose the valve seat and washer. Examine valve for grit, put in new washer, replace, and screw up.

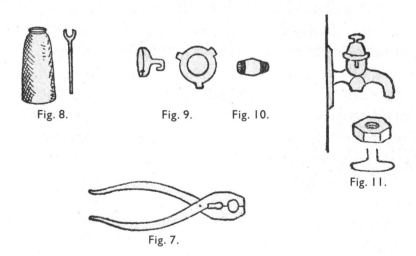

Fig. 8.

Fig. 9.   Fig. 10.

Fig. 11.

Fig. 7.

Sash Windows

Sash Lines are attached at one end to the frame containing the glass of the window, and at the other to a count weight (Fig. 12.), which enables the window to be easily opened and to keep open without having to insert a prop.

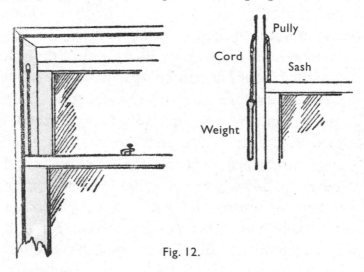

Fig. 12.

To replace Broken or Weak Cords. First, remove the beading on the side where the broken cord is. The window can then be swung out. In some windows, in more modern buildings, the beading is not nailed down, but fastened with hinges, so that it can be turned back. When the window is swung out, the board on which the window slides up and down is naturally exposed. At first sight, this board appears to be in one piece, but, on closer examination, it will be seen that it is cut across near the bottom. One or two taps with a hammer on this piece of cut board will remove it, and the weight will be found in the cavity left. It is a simple matter then to renew the cord, fasten it to the sash, pass it over the pulley and fasten the weight. There is, of course, a weight on each side of the window, and, if the top and bottom are both made to open, there will be two weights, one on the top half and one on the bottom half on each side.

Door Fastenings

The faults found in these will be chiefly knobs coming off spindle, and catch sticking inside case (Fig. 13.) after door has been opened. To repair the former, the small screw (A) to be found in the neck of the knob will require tightening, or, if lost or worn, replacing.

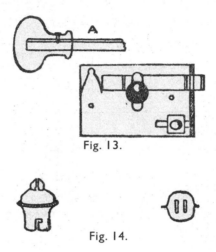

Fig. 13.

Fig. 14.

    The catch may stick either on account of the spring being worn out or broken, or through being clogged with dust and want of a little oil.

    To repair, remove knob and spindle (Fig. 14.), unscrew the case from door, remove the plate on inside by taking out the countersunk screw, taking note how the bolt, spring and lever are placed, and clean out or renew spring as required.

Replacing Electric Light Bulbs

This will not offer any difficulty, and is done very much the same way that an inverted mantle is put on.

Hanging Pictures and Curtains

It is impossible to give any set rules for these, as so much depends on the room and lighting. Only general hints can be given, and with respect to the pictures, the following may be useful. If the picture is to hang low or on a level with the eye, the angle made by the frame and wall will have to be very small; if hung high, the angle will have to be increased. This is accomplished by fixing the cord hooks; the further down on the frame of the picture these are, the more will the top of the picture come away from the wall (Fig.15.).

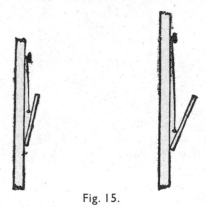

Fig. 15.

Should shadows be prominent, it sometimes adds greatly to the effect if the light from window or gas is so placed in relation to the picture, as to give or add to the impression that the shadows are caused thereby. As a general rule, also, a dark subject will be seen to better advantage on a well-lighted wall, and vice versa.

With curtains, first ascertain how these are required to "hang". and, bearing this in mind, fix on the most convenient

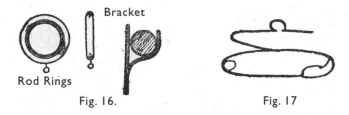

Rod Rings

Bracket

Fig. 16.   Fig. 17

place for the rod brackets, which are usually fixed screws.

On the curtain poles will be found a number of rings with pins attached. Divide these according to the number of curtains, unhook the pins and fix evenly to top of curtain; this done, hook the pins in rings again, and loop up the lower portion of the curtain to obtain the best appearance (Figs. 16. and 17.).

Portiere Roads are treated in a similar manner to above.

Laying Carpets

If "squares", does not present much difficulty. If the furniture is in the room, the carpet should be rolled, as this saves a good deal of lifting. Clear the centre of the floor, and get the carpet into proper position at the part. Now, take the edge which will come under the heavy piece, and roll towards the middle, until the unrolled portion can be fixed (being clear of furniture). Now, get the roll of carpet close up to whatever it has to pass under and, when this is raised up, give the roll a smart push, when the carpet will lie almost ready for fixing. Repeat above with other side, stretching out any waves.

Small Repairs to Furniture

Broken chair backs. When these are the result of the wood-plugs drying in, glue a thin wafer round the socket and, when this is dry and set, refix the plugs with glue, also. To use nails will in a big majority of cases only mean more repairs, owing to the wood cracking. When the wood is split, a better job is made of the repair if the damaged part is cut away and the end thus left finished with Z ends. Make a piece to match that cutaway, making the ends fit into parts already prepared, then glue. (Treat broken legs in same way.)

Sharpening Knives.

On the ordinary "steel", hold steel firmly in left hand, point upwards. Take knife in other hand and draw the edge down the steel, from heel of blade to point, treating one side and then the other (go and watch the local butcher). If the edge is so dull that something more effective than the steel is required, a rough stone (hone) or grindstone should be used. Leather, on which emery powder has been sprinkled, is effective, also.

Fig. 18.

HEALTHY MAN BADGE

A Scout must:

1. Know the importance of keeping the heart, lungs, skin, teeth, feet and stomach and the organs of special senses (eyes, ears and nose) in good order and the principal dangers to be guarded against.

2. Give general rules governing eating, drinking, breathing, sleeping, cleanliness and exercising; give proof that he has kept fit by the observance ot these rules for at least 12 months.

3. Know the dangers incurred in the use of tobacco and the danger of overtraining the body, and the continuing use of one form of exercise.

PART I

Heart

Importance of keeping Heart in good order: If the heart is not kept in good order, the valve become strained and do not do their duty, the blood partly flows backwards instead of forwards, or does not get driven through the body at the correct rate and in correct quantities; this all throws much too great a strain on the heart, and it either gradually or suddenly becomes incapable of performing its duty of pumping the blood through the body.

The strain may partially prevent the heart doing its work, in which case the person may become a permanent invalid, only fit for very little work, and utterly unfit for joining in any games, or perhaps even such simple exercise as a good walk. It means no football, no cricket, no cycling, swimming or any of the things in which a healthy Scout delights. In case of the strain becoming suddenly too great, the heart may stop beating altogether and thus cause death.

Lungs

Importance of keeping Lungs in good order: If the lungs are not fully developed, or if a lung becomes partially diseased or unable to do its work, the blood will not get the full amount of oxygen, which will make for ill-health, or the disease may be carried by the blood to other parts of the body. Under-developed lungs cause a flat, underdeveloped chest.

The Air you breathe in must be Pure: The best way to ensure this is to keep the window open at all times; every breath you give out is full of impurities, and if there are no means whereby these impurities can escape from the room and fresh air enter, the impure air is re-breathed with very bad effect. Especially when a number of people are sitting in a warm room with the gas lit, or when in bed with the door closed for eight or ten hours, must the window be open.

The window should be open from 3 inches to 18 inches, according to weather and inclination; but it must always be open. It is best to be open at the top, as the warm, impure air is lighter than the pure, and it consequently rises and escapes at the opening.

All kinds of germs can be taken into the lungs and infect the body therefrom. The one which requires the greatest care to prevent gaining a footing is the germ of consumption (tuberculosis). Consumption occurs most often among those who do not have plenty of clean, pure, fresh air.Consumption is very difficult to cure and is so dangerous that every effort must be made not to get it; the methods of prevention are simple – fresh air, open windows, deep breathing and breathing through the nose. Sunlight and open air; out Scouting with the Troop or long country walks on Saturday afternoons and holidays, instead of playing about the house or in close streets – these are the helps you can give.

Skin

The chief use of the skin is to help (along with some of the other organs) to get rid of impurities from the body; these impurities escape through the pores in the skin in the form of perspiration; these pores are tiny holes in the skin, so small that a sixpence could cover thousands of them.

To keep in thorough health, these pores must never be allowed to become blocked, or the waste materials of the body cannot get out, and ill-health will result. To prevent this, keep the skin clean. A hot bath at least once a week is absolutely necessary. Every Scout should take a pride in keeping his body clean; not only the parts which are seen, but every part of the body.

In addition to the regular hot bath, the skin should be cleaned daily. The daily cleansing of the skin may take the form either of a morning cold bath or a cold sponge-down. The cold bath does not in wintertime require to be dead cold; the chill may be taken off by the addition of a little warm water. Nor need a long time be spent in the bath: to step in, rub the body all over with a rough loofah or piece of towelling, sit down and let the water cover the body, rub down again and then jump out, is all that is necessary. Scouts who have not been in the habit of taking cold baths can start them gradually by at first putting in a little extra warm water, and by not actually sitting down in the water for the first few days.

Remember that after either the cold tub or the rub-down, a vigorous towelling stimulates the circulation of the blood, and is an important part of the treatment. Never take a hot bath in the morning or when going out into the street, unless you finish with a cold plunge or a cold spray, as the hot water opens the pores, and if they remain open in cold air there is a great risk of catching cold. After being overheated by violent exercise of any sort, it is advisable to undress, rub the skin dry and, if possible, put on clean underclothing; otherwise, there is here again a big chance of catching cold. When very hot, do not stand in a draught.

If you get your feet wet, or get soaked through to the skin, change into dry shoes and stockings, or, if necessary, dry clothing altogether, at the very first opportunity; it is not the getting wet that causes colds so much as remaining in wet clothing.

Teeth

In order to be healthy it is essential that the teeth should be kept in good order. Decayed teeth mean a dirty mouth, and a dirty mouth means ill-health. Clean teeth do not decay. Decayed teeth mean poisons entering the system and consequent want of fitness. Your teeth must be brushed at least once every day, preferably at night just before going to bed. If your teeth are not in good order, you cannot masticate your food properly, and it does not digest easily or fully. Go to the dentist occasionally, even if you have no pain, as decay is best attended to and the tooth filled before the stage at which you feel the tooth hurting.

Feet

The first thing in care of the feet is to keep them perfectly clean; in all weathers, but especially in summer, they must be scrubbed and attended to regularly. The next thing is to wear boots which are big enough; if you wear boots which are large enough (but not so large that the foot moves about inside the boot and gets chafed), there is small risk of getting corns. Do not try to look fashionable with pointed-toed boots; rather, look sensible with broad toes, to allow your feet to lie in a natural and comfortable position.

In hot weather, a little boracic acid powder dusted into the stockings will keep the feet dry and pleasant. If you are going for a long walk or march, do not put on new boots, but wear a pair that have been well broken in to your feet.

When walking a lot or marching, change your stockings every second day, if possible.

Eyes

The great thing in care of the eyes is not to strain them; never read in the failing evening light; never read in the sun or artificial light facing you. Do not concentrate the gaze on any small object for too long, as this also strains the eyes.

Should you have any difficulty in reading, or find things hazy at all, tell your parents at once, as immediate attention will often save years of wearing glasses, and perhaps in some cases prevent partial or total blindness.

Ears

Keep them clean. Do not push any sharp-pointed instrument or pencil into them. If you have to be near any extremely loud noises, put cotton wool in the ears first, as otherwise there is a risk of the drums being broken by the tremendous vibration.

Nose

Your nose is meant for breathing through, so always use it instead of your mouth for that purpose. The nose is full of small, fine hairlike processes, whose duty is to catch dust etc., on its way in and prevent it getting carried to the lungs. Another reason is that there is a very large blood supply to the nose (you can discover this for yourself by having a fight), the purpose of is to warm the air before it enters the lungs; if you breathe through your mouth, the air enters cold, and there is a much larger risk of your getting a cold in the chest than if you breathe through the nose. Mouth breathers have generally a silly, stupid look (keep your eyes open and you will see that this is so), and mouth breathing causes, in many cases, ugly, irregular, prominent teeth; it also causes adenoids, which have to be removed by operation.

Like the rest of a Scout's body, your nose must be kept perfectly clean.

Stomach

Most of the illnesses which people suffer from (it is often said) come from want of care of the stomach. The ills arise from two causes: the putting in of food and the taking it out.

The putting in will. be treated under the head of "Eating", in Part II. The taking out means, of course, the clearing of the bowel regularly. This should be done at a regular time every day, preferably the morning immediately after breakfast; but to keep in good health the bowel must be emptied every day without fail, otherwise the waste matter of the body, instead of passing away will be partially re-absorbed into the body and cause all sorts of illnesses.

PART II

Eating

Eat at regular times only. Do not eat between meals. Eat enough to satisfy your hunger without giving yourself a feeling of uncomfortable fullness. Eat as much green stuff (vegetables such as cabbage and lettuce) as you can get with your meals.

Do not eat too much sweet food; sweets in small quantities are quite good for you, but do not take too many.

Do not eat too much ripe raw fruit, and never eat any unripe fruit.

If you are at work and cannot get home for your midday meal, don't eat scones and cakes and tea. A little meat and potatoes will do you far more good; and, if you cannot get that, rather have a plate of soup and some bread than tea and scones. Tea and scones in the middle of the day make you soft and flabby, gives your skin a bad colour, and get you out of training.

The most important thing of all is to eat slowly; masticate your food well; bite every mouthful until it is thoroughly chewed and broken up, for the stomach cannot digest big pieces of food (even soft food), and the undigested pieces irritate the lining of the stomach and cause what is called indigestion.

Drinking

Drink lots of pure, clean cold water. The water must be pure; if you have any doubt about it, boil it for ten minutes, allow it to get cold, and pour off into a clean vessel, leaving a small amount (at the foot of the boiling can), which should be thrown away.

Lemonade made from fresh lemons is much better than the "gassy" kind. Ordinary lemonade, gingerbeer etc. should only be taken in small quantities. Scouts should never take alcohol in any form (see below).

When to drink: Drink cold water before going to bed at night (unless you find that it makes you go to the lavatory too often); drink cold water in the morning when you get up (before breakfast).

Pure cold water drunk during the day will wash out your stomach and intestines, help to clear your bowels, keep you clean inside, and keep you healthy.

Drink at the end of eating rather than while eating, because drinking while you are eating prevents the flow of saliva and thus hinders digestion.

When not to drink: Do not drink when you are very hot, rather cool down a little first; if you require a drink while hot take a small quantity only.

Don't drink while on the march. When marching or cycling there is a great temptation to drink at short halts, but this prevents you making good progress thereafter, and also causes you to get more thirsty. Never drink "fizzy" or "gassy" drinks while on the march.

Cocoa is better for you than tea. Cocoa is a food; tea has no value for body-building at all, neither has coffee. Tea should be taken once a day only, certainly no more than twice.

Sleeping

Get lots of sleep; until you are fully grown you require at least nine hours actual sleep (not merely nine hours in bed, but nine hours' sleep).

Sleep with your window open from the top all year round. Sleep with your gas out, or at least in only a tiny peep.

Take off all your underclothing at night; you must let your underclothing air and the perspiration of the daytime dry, and this cannot be done if you keep any part of your day underclothing on at night. It may seem rather cold at first, but once you have got into the way of sleeping in only your pyjamas or nightshirt you will never want to go back to the old unsanitary way.

Keep your head well above the bedclothes. Always sleep with your mouth closed; this will, among other things, prevent you waking with a dry, sour, furry taste in your mouth.

Sleep with your feet stretched right down, and not with your body curled up.

Cleanliness

The only thing which remains to be added is that all underclothing must be changed as often as possible – it is impossible to say how often, as this will necessarily depend to some extent on family circumstances; but there is no excuse for any Scout not to keep his body and underclothing clean.

PART III

Dangers incurred in the use of Tobacco

Smoking is not an evil thing, but it is a very bad thing – a bad thing for your health.

Smoking prevents your growth, not the growing tall so much (though it often affects that), but the growth of your heart and lungs. You have seen from the previous part of this article the importance of keeping your heart and lungs in good order – well, all doctors are agreed that even if it does you no harm when you are fully grown (and some doctors say it does you harm even then, certainly if you smoke much it does), smoking while your body and internal organs are growing is very bad for your heart, your lungs, your stomach and your eyesight.

See what the Chief Scout says in *Scouting for Boys* about the effect on your powers of smell and sight: "Your father may smoke – well, what about it? He is fully grown, and it cannot prevent the development of his heart and lungs; but that does not apply to you. For the same reason that you go to bed earlier than your father, because the growing body requires more care; similarly, to assist that growing body, you should not smoke."

What other reason would we have to worry you not to smoke? Consider then, and if you are convinced that smoking is bad for you, have enough determination, be man enough, be Scout enough not to smoke even when "offered it by the other chap".

Dangers incurred in the use of Alcohol

Alcohol is not a food. All that it does is to send part of the brain to sleep and thus cause things for a short time only to seem better than they are; because part of the brain is asleep, hunger for a short time may seem to be less; or, in time of worry, if a person partakes of alcohol the worry for a short time may seem to disappear. That is the whole effect of partaking of beer, wine or spirits; but rapidly the effect wears off and leaves the person in a worse state than before the drink was taken, because the body and brain are now less able to resist hunger, cold or worry.

Spirit in any form – except occasionally when ordered by a doctor – is an enemy of the heart, of the brain, of the stomach, and all the organs of special senses; nor would it be so bad if it could be kept under control, but unfortunately with many people even a small quantity of liquor excites them to a desire for more and more, ending in a state of being fuddled or even completely drunk.

The Danger In Overtraining the Body

The danger of overtraining the body is that you may strain yourself. You may strain your muscles, your lungs or your heart.

A strained muscle is painful but not dangerous; rest and some embrocation will put it all right, but not so with a strained lung or a strained heart.

Don't overdo it is the best advice to avoid straining. If you are going in .for training or for games, start gently and gradually work It up. (Remember not to smoke while you are in training-athletes never smoke except in the off season).

In all your games and exercises, don't overdo it – Softee, softee, catch monkey!

HORSEMAN BADGE

A Scout must:

1. In the case of light horses, know how to ride at all paces, and jump an ordinary fence on horseback.

How to saddle and bridle a horse correctly.

How to harness a horse correctly in single and double harness, and be able to drive single and pair.

2. In the case of heavy draught horses or vanners, know how to harness them in single and double harness for cart, van and wagon, and in chains; and in either alternative:

(a) Know how to water and feed, and groom, his horse properly.

(b) Know the evil of bearing and hame rems and ill-fitting harness.

(c) Be able to detect common ailments and lameness.

(d) Be able to keep and clean harness properly.

The natural paces of the horse are the walk, the trot and the gallop. The canter is not natural to a horse in its wild state but is acquired after being broken in.

In the walk, each leg is lifted up and put down separately, one after the other. The print of the hind foot is generally a few inches in front of that of the forefoot.

In the trot the two legs of opposite sides are moved exactly together, and touch the ground at the same moment.

In the gallop the horse makes a succession of leaps, during a part of which all the legs are off the ground, and, as the feet come to the ground, they strike it in regular succession.

The following terms are used by horsemen:

The left side is called the near side.

The right side is called the off side.

A hand is 4 inches (the height of a horse is always measured by hands).

The upper part of the neck is called the crest.

The ridge of bone in front of the saddle is called the withers.

The part between the saddle and the tail is called the croup.

The bony points on each side of the breast are called the shoulder points.

Between these and the withers is called the line of the shoulder.

In the fore legs the two divisions are called arm and cannon.

In the hind legs the two divisions are called thigh and cannon.

Above the arm and cannon of the fore leg is the elbow joint, and between them the knee joint.

In the hind leg the corresponding joints are called the stifle and hock.

Below these on both legs are the upper and lower pasterns, then the coronet, which is the ring between the leg and the foot, and lastly there is the hoof.

A good horseman should personally supervise the saddling and binding of his horse, and before mounting should see that the girths and bridles are properly adjusted.

To Mount

Stand at the shoulder of the horse, on the near side (that is the horse's left side), with the rider's left side towards the horse's shoulder. Catch the reins with the left hand drawing them short enough to *feel* the mouth and at the same time twist a lock of the mane in the fingers, so as to steady the hand then place the left foot in the stirrup. Spring up off the fight foot, at the same time gripping the saddle with the right hand, raise the body till right leg is in line with the left, then, after a momentary pause, throw the right leg over the horse, keeping the toe down and heel elevated. The right hand releases its hold, and the body settles into the centre of the saddle, and the right foot is placed in the stirrup.

To Dismount

The process is exactly the reverse of mountmg. Shorten the reins and hold them in the left hand, with a lock of the mane. Take the right foot out of the stirrup, and throw the right leg over the back of the horse until it is level with the left leg; lower the body to the ground, and take left foot out of the stirrup.

The rider should always sit square to the front, neither shoulder being in advance of the other, the loins slightly arched inwards without stiffness, the elbows close to the side but not constrained, the knees pressed against the padded part of the saddle in front of the stirrupleathers, the toes very slightly towards the foot resting on the stirrup; the inside of the stirrup should be opposite the ball of the big toe, and the outside opposite the little toe. The heels should be lowered as far as possible beneath the level of the toe. The main point, however, is to obtain a good grasp of the saddle with the knees. Straw should be spread out at night, and well tossed about with the pitchfork. Care, however, should be taken not to put any of the straw below the manger, as this encourages the horse to eat his bedding, a habit which. once acquired, is very difficult to get rid of, and results in colic and indigestion.

SADDLE (MOUNTED)

1. Top part is called the seat.
2. The parts attached to it at the top of the stirrup leathers are called skirts.

3. The pieces corning down the sides are called the flaps.

4. The cushion in the inside of the saddle is called the panel. The web straps with buckles at each end are called the girths.

5. The straps which hold the stirrups are called stirrup leathers.

6. The irons for supporting the feet are called stirrup irons.

This consists of 1. bridle; 2. reins; 3. neck collar; 4. hames; 5. traces; 6. saddle; 7. back-band; 8. shaft-loops; 9. crupper; 10. cross-strap;. 11, Britchen web; 12. shaft-straps.

Yoking requires to be seen and explained whilst being done.

DRIVING HARNESS

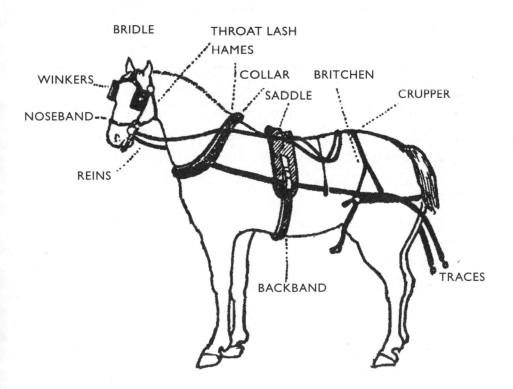

RIDING BRIDLE

1. The strap going over the head at the back of the ears, and split at each end, is called the head-stall.
2. The strap on the brow, on front of the ears is called the front.
3. The strap from head-stall down cheek to bit is called the cheek.
4. The strap from head-stall round the throat is called the throat lash.
5. The top rein, or the one nearest the wick, is called the driving rein.
6. The bottom one is called the check rein.

Watering

Clean, pure water is essential for horses. Serious illnesses have been contracted by drinking water contaminated with sewage etc. Horses should never be allowed to drink at public watering troughs, as dieases such as glanders have often been traced to this source. A constant supply of fresh water should be at the head of the stall, so that the horse may drink whenever it likes. When a horse is overheated, however, it should not be allowed an unlimited quantity;1 to 2 quarts is sufficient.

Driving

In Britain the Rule of the Road is keep to the left in meeting other vehicles, and leave vehicles on the left in passing them.

The Rule of the Road is a paradox quite;
If you go to the left you will surely be right;
If you go to the right, you go wrong.

It should be remembered that on the Continent and in America the rule is exactly reversed. The law there is *drive to the right.*

The driver should be careful to keep his feet well before him, with his knees as straight and firm as possible. so that if the horse should fall he will not be thrown forward out of the vehicle. He should also sit square, with elbow held naturally close to his side. If his left thumb is pointed towards the horse's head, his elbow will be kept in the proper position.

The forefinger of the left hand should be placed between the reins, and then both the reins should be grasped by all the other fingers. The near or left rein is held firmly against the forefinger with the thumb. In this way the left rein may be pulled by itself, by holding it firmly by the thumb, and allowing the off or right rein to slip through the fingers.

INTERPRETER BADGE

A Scout must be able to carry on a simple conversation, write a simple letter on-subject given by examiner, read and translate a passage from a book or newspaper, in either Esperanto or any language that is not that of his own country.

LETTER-WRITING IS A USEFUL SKILL

LAUNDRYMAN BADGE

A Scout must wash and finish garments of cotton and flannel, including starching and "getting up" a shirt.

Laundry work is roughly divided into two classes of goods:
Animal and vegetable fibres,
Flannel and cotton articles,
because what is good for the one is destructive to the other.

Flannel: The temperature should not exceed blood heat, 98°F; they must be washed off quickly and not allowed to lie about. No soda or alkali must be used, nor must flannels be rubbed too much in contact with one another or shrinkage will occur. With flannel goods an oil soap is used, preferably a potash soap, and should not be thoroughly washed out of the garment.

Chip up some soap and dissolve by boiling. Make up solution with warm water in a bucket, 98°F, and squeeze garment through the soapy suds several times (say five). Any extra dirty portions are put on a flat surface and scrubbed with a brush, e.g., back of neck, cuffs etc.

Underclothing and socks are turned outside in before being washed. Black socks are best washed by themselves to keep ooze from speckling them.

Give flannels a wash out of soap liquor and squeeze tightly. Dry off.

Silk goods are washed like flannels but require great care. A little methylated spirits in last wash improves lustre.

Cotton Goods: Steep well for 6 hours, overnight or before washing. Steeping saves half the labour, dissolving all soluble and sugary impurities, blood stains etc. On taking out of the steep, wash well in warm soap liquor, scrubbing where necessary. When well washed, squeeze tightly and put into another soap liquor to boil for halfanhour. Care must be taken that suds are present, or lime soap will be precipitated on the garments, making black specks which are very hard to remove. Lime specks chiefly occur in hard water, i.e. water from a spring or chalky ground.

After boiling, rinse out well in cold water.

Starched goods must be well boiled in order to get rid of old starch and thereby ensure a good colour.

It is imperative for good results to wash in luke-warm water before boiling, or albuminous matter from the skin, perspiration, organic salts, blood etc. will be coagulated from the sudden heat before being removed from the garment. A good example of coagulation is the white of an egg (albumenoid matter). Every Scout knows how hard it becomes in boiling.

Boiling also sterilises the goods thoroughly, which is very important; whereas, flannels have to depend upon the nascent steam generated in ironing, which is also very good.

Curd or tallow soaps are used for cotton goods, with a little washing soda.

Ironing: Flannels are dried before ironing. The dry garment is smoothed out by the action of the steam generated from a wet piece of muslin placed on top of the garment and ironed with a moderately hot iron.

Silks are ironed wet with an iron of medium temperature.

Cotton goods are dried, damped slightly with water, rolled

up to allow damp to permeate all through, and then ironed on moist slate.

Finishing Operations: The iron is kept very hot, and must be cleaned with a damp rag and surface lightly "waxed". The goods to be ironed are in a half-dry condition. If dry, scorch marks will result. The goods are ironed on top of a blanket. Woollen articles, semmits, pants, shirts etc. are not starched, neither are ordinary cotton or linen shirts, handkerchiefs, scarves etc. Starched articles are chiefly confined to white stiff shirts and stiff collars. Collars are best starched in "cold water rice starch".

The collars are then starched in this mixture (after washing) by rubbing or kneading well in the starch. Squeeze well and rub with a dry cloth, and collar can now be ironed.

First, endeavour to set the collar free from creases, pressing on each side with the iron. When partially dry, more pressure is brought to bear, increasing pressure and friction until a gloss is produced. The collar is folded and given a round shape by ironing on the inside and pulling each free end over the iron.

The breast of a white stiff shirt is starched in the same way as the collar. Iron the inside of the yoke first, then the outside, then iron the neckband. Now iron the back of the shirt. This is done by folding it down the middle and ironing each side. Now iron the sleeves. The breast and cuffs are next ironed, somewhat in the same manner as a collar, only on a larger and more skilful scale, being particular to remove creases. When almost dry, the shirt is polished by rubbing hard with a round-nosed or polishing iron.

LEATHER WORKER BADGE

A Scout must have a knowledge of tanning and curing; and either:
Be able to sole and heel a pair of boots, sewn or nailed, and
generally repair boots and shoes; or
Be able to dress a saddle, repair traces, stirrup leathers etc., and
know the various parts of harness.

Leather consists of the skins of animals, which have been cured or tanned so as to prevent the decomposition which would otherwise take place and, also, to give greatly increased strength and toughness, and to make the material waterproof.

There are three ways in which the skins are prepared:

The most important, is with tan bark or other vegetable substances containing tannin. This process is called tanning.

By tawing with alum, bichromate of potash or other minerals.

By soaking the raw skin in oil. This is called shamoying.

Large skins, such as those of cattle or horses, are called hides; small ones, such as sheep, goats etc. are called skins.

The skins of all animals can be made into leather, but the skins usually employed are those of animals which are killed for other purposes, such as food etc. The principal source from which a tanner gets the skins is, therefore, the slaughter-house.

MASON BADGE

A Scout must lay at least four courses of a straight wall with a corner, in addition to the foundation and damp course; must make mortar and understand the use of a plumb line and trowel.

The information required for this badge is best got by practical experience, and the Scout should get on good terms with a mason at some neighbouring building in course of erection.

Before considering the tests, the following remarks should be carefully noted.

Foundations

A stone wall of a building usually rests on a concrete foundation. This is to distribute the weight of the wall equally over the ground. The bottom of this foundation should be at least two feet below the surface of the ground, so as to be away from the attack of frost.

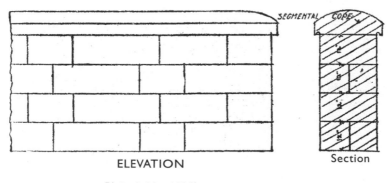

ELEVATION   Section

Plain Ashlar Wall

Dampcourse

Every wall of a building must have a damp-proof course throughout its entire thickness. This is to prevent dampness rising from the ground and so causing damage to walls etc. It is laid slightly above the surface of adjoining ground. The materials commonly used for this purpose are Caithness pavement slabs and slates.

Walls

Masonry walls may be classed either as:

Ashlar. This consists of large blocks of stone carefully worked so that the joints are generally 3/16th of an inch in thickness.

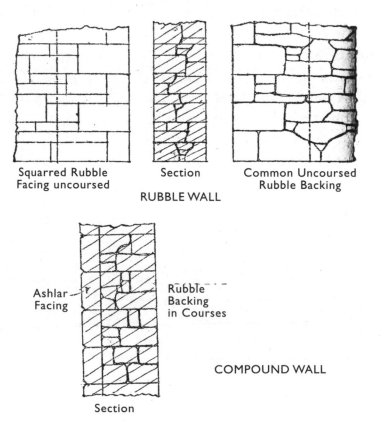

Squarred Rubble Facing uncoursed   Section   Common Uncoursed Rubble Backing

RUBBLE WALL

Ashlar Facing   Rubble Backing in Courses

COMPOUND WALL

Section

Rubble. This consists of small stones of irregular shape and hardly worked at all. The thickness of the joint in this class of work is about 3/8th of an inch.

To save expense, these two kinds of walls are generally combined. For instance, the front wall of a tenement would be built with ashlar facing and rubble backing (see above), while the back wall would be wholly of rubble.

The corner stones of walls are called quoins. These are usually built stronger than the rest of the wall, as the angle of the building depends on them for strength.

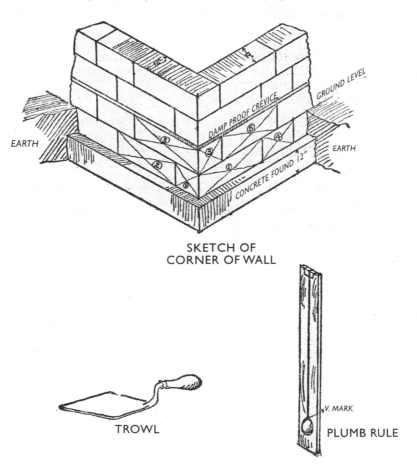

SKETCH OF
CORNER OF WALL

TROWL

PLUMB RULE

MASTER-AT-ARMS BADGE

A Scout must attain proficiency in two out of the following subjects: Single-Stick, Quarter-Staff, Fencing, Boxing, Ju-Jitsu, and Wrestling.

This is one of the most difficult badges to teach on paper. If possible, an instructor should be secured. The Scout who goes in for this badge should not scramble over it, but should try and benefit by it. He would do himself a great deal of good if he went on learning its different parts, or as many as possible, even after he has passed his examination. Whatever the special parts he takes for his badges, he will find, as he learns, that position and suppleness are the secrets of good fighting. Moving the feet is as essential to all of these arts as moving the hands. They all demand suppleness of the waist, and the tests for the badge might advantageously be supplemented with the demonstration of one or two simple waist exercises such as are given in the health part of *Scouting for Boys*.

Single-Sticks

The stick is made of ash, with a small pin in its thick end to keep it from slipping out of the hilt.

LEATHER GUARD

Hit with Leather Guard

The Hilt is made of wickerwork. It unfortunately very readily breaks. To obviate this ,soak it in water now and again; also, fit an extra guard on it. Pierce a hole about the thickness of the single-stick through a thick piece of leather (a piece of old lathes strap will do very well), pass it through till it is close against the hilt, and it will not only preserve the basket, but save your thumb from hard hits (see above).

Dress: A thick jacket (leather if possible); a padded gauntlet glove, a thick mask and a leather sporran or apron.

Position on Guard is the same as in fencing, with two exceptions: 1. The right arm is straightened out, fingernails to the right, cutting edge and hilt upwards. Stick and arm in a straight line.

2. The left hand is clenched and kept behind the body.

The Advance is the same as in foils, the right foot moves first.

The Retire, also, the left foot moves first.

The Lunge should be made simultaneously with the cut. Straight point lunges not allowed.

The Recover from the lunge is effected by pressing with the right foot on the ground, the body regaining the perpendicular of guard.

The Re-attack: After lunging, bring the left foot up into guard, then relunge. After the last lunge, recover in the ordinary way.

The Cuts: There are six principal cuts:
Upwards and Undercuts.
1. *Prime* at the opponent's left flank.
2. *Second* at the opponent's right flank.

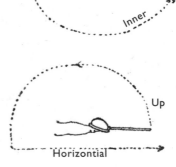

Upwards and Horizontal.
3. Tierce at the opponent's right shoulder.
4. Quarte at the opponent's left shoulder.

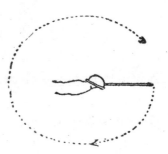

Downwards and Downcuts.
5. Quinte at the opponent's left cheek.
6. Sixte at the opponent's right cheek.

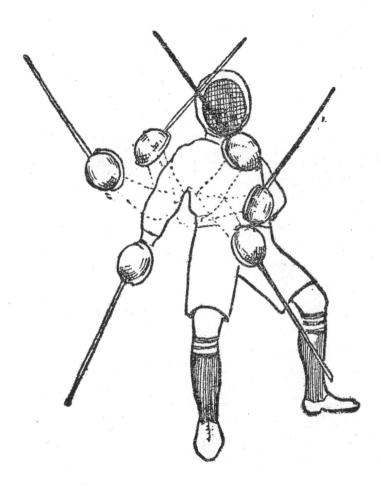

There are six parries corresponding to these. They are always affected with circular motion of the hand and blade, counterclockwise for the right-hand parries, clockwise for the left. The figure above will demonstrate them in a better way than any description to the novice.

He must remember to "push" his parries, or he will suffer a "broken guard" if his opponent is at all muscular.

Boxing

The art of boxing appeals instinctively to boys, perhaps because no appurtenances are required other than those with which we are adorned by nature, in order to indulge in a bout of fisticuffs. It also has its advantages as a means of defence when one is harassed by unwelcome attentions on a lonely road. But apart from these considerations, it is to be recommended to all Scouts as a healthy recreation and an excellent means of teaching them to keep their temper at all times, and to be cool and collected even when "hard hit".

To many, boxing consists in facing an opponent with one arm before the other, and in getting in as many hits at their opponent as possible with a minimum of injury to themselves. With this idea as a basis, a boy sometimes endeavours to make up for his lack of science by practising the art of boxing with an equally ignorant opponent, until he imagines himself to be a luminary of the prize ring by reason of his having overcome his opponent's guard. Unfortunately, for the end which he has in view, however, the best way to become a bad boxer is follow the promptings of nature in the matters of hitting and guarding, and to learn without a master. A bad style in boxing, as in most other things, is very difficult to "unlearn", and few ever lay claim to much success in the boxing world who have not learned the art early, under an efficient master. In the event of such a person not being readily obtainable, quite a lot can be picked up by the study of books, and from these one can at least be taught those things which one must not do when face to face with an opponent in the ring, with nothing but a pair of gloves with which to keep him off.

Boxing is the art of self-defence, and to be able to defend oneself is even more important than being able to injure an antagonist. If an adversary can be wearied out in trying to get past your defence, it makes it much easier, when the time comes, to get past his. The first method of defence has already been referred to, that of retreating, and as has been said, unless this retreat is carried out in good order by moving the right leg first, or springing back on both, it may end in a rout. It is, however, one of the safest methods of defence, as it gets you beyond the reach of your opponent's hit. You can retreat in this fashion quicker than your opponent can advance upon you, which ensures your safety for the moment. The next method to be commented on is that of ducking, which is often very effective, but is decidedly more dangerous than that of retreating in good order. It consists in suddenly bending the head, and, if necessary, the body as well, in order to escape a blow.

On guard. Ducking to the right.

It is, however, a very dangerous device to use more than once or twice against an opponent who knows anything about boxing, as it will induce him to give effect to the hit known as the 'upper cut', which means that with his free hand he will give an upward hit at your head, which you cannot well guard. The method of defence by ducking may be effectively used in combination with several kinds of counterstrokes, which will be explained later. Allied in idea to ducking, is the defence by side step, which requires considerable practice in order to be neatly done. If it is clumsily manoeuvred, instead of being a means of defence it leaves the learner open to a blow from his opponent's left. To achieve the side step, the weight of the body must suddenly be placed on the left foot, and the right foot lifted well out to the right, the left foot following it quickly and being put in its proper position in front of the right. This leaves your opponent facing nothing, and may enable you to get through his left upper arm guard, as well as to escape from his pressing attentions. A side step to the left may be made in a somewhat similar way, but it should not be used unless under exceptional circumstances, as it is not good policy to work round to the left in boxing.

Side slipping.

Slipping.

The means of defence mentioned hitherto have all been by escape. There still remain, defence by guarding with the arm, and by means of countering. To take the first of these, the right arm is the guard arm, though, of course, both must be used. The position taken up on commencing a round, that is the "on guard", is the correct defence for a blow aimed at your body. To guard a blow from your adversary's left, the right fist should be raised till about level with the eyebrows, the elbow straightened, and the knuckles turned inward, exposing the muscles of the forearm to receive the blow.

Guarding with the left.   Leading off.

This guard is also very effective in dealing with a round hit, especially if your elbow is pointed sharply outwards, as it catches your antagonist in a soft part of his forearm, and will probably deter him from attempting any more round hits. The last defence to be mentioned is that by a counterhit. In boxing, great advantage goes to the man with a long reach, for by means of his length of arm he can keep his opponent off, and get in hits while his adversary cannot reach him. By taking full advantage of his reach, and by keeping his right arm ready for emergencies, his opponent is disconcerted, and so long as the arm keeps pointed out, so long is he safe. It is well for a beginner to practise these methods of defence for a very considerable time before he thinks of becoming the aggressor, and he should not try to make a single hit until he gets confidence in his own defence, and is able to guard himself properly.

When this result has been achieved, the beginner may begin to interest himself in the various points of attack. The first thing, naturally, to take his attention, should be the lead off, and, until he becomes proficient in this, he should make it his sole hit.

The principal idea is to be able to make the hit from as safe a distance as possible; that is, the fist should just be able to reach the object aimed at with as little waste of reach as possible. To do so requires a good deal of practice, preferably with a punching ball. One very important point in leading off is to be able to recover after having delivered the blow. Recovery, of course, is made by springing back with the left leg, and the beginner must be very careful not to expect an impulse for the recovery from the object struck. For leading off, the left arm should be used almost exclusively, as it is both a difficult and a dangerous proceeding to lead off with the right.

A few general precepts may, however, be mentioned, which will doubtless prove of use.

When on guard, you should not be within striking distance of your opponent, but should be able to reach him by advancing the left foot and leading off.

Having once led off, it is best to get out of distance at once, and the lead off hit itself should be made quickly so that your opponent has not time to guess your intention and to deliver a counterblow.

If your opponent is taller, then he will get the best of the fight, unless you do most of the leading off, and show him that you are a quicker and a cleverer man.

If your adversary is heavier, your aim should be to "draw" him as much as possible, and to counter him at every opportunity, so that his weight, by coming unexpectedly against your fists, may tell against him.

If a certain hit or ruse succeeds, do not attempt to repeat it too soon, for your opponent may have learned his lesson and be shy the next time.

If you are getting the best of your adversary, never be rash and try daring hits. You have little to gain and everything to lose.

Keep your hands and your mouth shut, but never your eyes. If your mouth is open you may get your jaw dislocated.

Do not jump about, fussing with the arms and moving the feet, in the hopes of perplexing your adversary. You only tire yourself without bothering him.

The heaviest blow you can get in is on an advancing opponent; the lightest when he is retreating.

Do not get your legs close together, or put the right foot in front of the left, or get your legs crossed.

If possible, make your opponent retreat to his left, as this is always disconcerting to him.

If there is a strong light shining, get your back to it when fighting, as you will be better able to judge distance and to see your opponent's movements than if you are facing it.

It is much better not to make a hit at all than to make a short hit and find yourself out of reach of your opponent. You must learn to judge distance by practice, with a punching ball.

Right-hand counter.

Left-hand counter.

Cross-counter body blow.

Ju-Jitsu

Preparation: Ju-Jitsu is not only a style of wrestling and of scientific self-defence, it also implies a long training. As the Scout "Master-at-Arms" Badge only requires an average standard, and as space is exacting, I shall confine myself to giving only a few of the principal points of Ju-Jitsu.

Before a Scout learns to wrestle, he must make himself physically fit by the exercises given in *Scouting for Boys*; then he must practise various falls, locks and throws.

The Breakfall is the chief of these. He must learn to fall without hurting himself.

Practice 1. Lie on your back; lean over to the left whilst bringing the arm across your body; strike the ground with the whole arm at about 45° to the line of body, and roll over onto it. Then bring the left arm across and repeat the exercise with this arm. Keep this up for some time.

Practice 2. From a squatting position, fall backwards. Strike the ground with one arm just before the body does and roll over onto the other. Alternate arm each time.

Practice 3. From a standing position, fall back, keeping the head well forward. In the same way as in Practice 2, roll over from one arm to the other, changing arms at every fall.

Forward Breakfall: Practice 4. From a standing position, fall forward. Keep perfectly rigid and do not bend the knees. Just before the body strikes, raise the forearm (as in half-salute) and strike with both forearms and the palms of the hands at the same time.

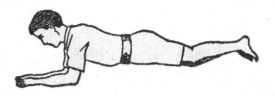

A Scout must also learn some anatomy. He will have to reason out for himself the various leverings, if I may so call them, which are applied to the weak parts of the human frame and constitute the science of Ju-Jitsu. He must also learn to quickly find and apply his fingers to the nervecentres.

The Nerve Centres: The ones most useful (or vice versa) to the Ju-Jitsuist are in the hand; in the forearm, under the arm, in the calf and under the nose (see below).

When pressure is applied to the four first, a dull numbing pain is felt. This should be quite sufficient to make a wrestler loose a hold. The last one can be used in self-defence when a chest bug is being applied. Free one arm and strike an upward cutting blow under the nose with the edge of the hand. This small blow, with the application of the foot behind the foremost leg of the attacker, will often knock him over.

Note: The crosses on figures denote nerve-centres.

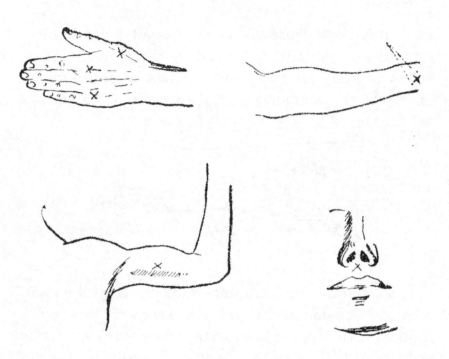

Wrestling

Many people consider that wrestling is too violent an exercise for boys. This is quite erroneous. It is one of the finest methods for developing a boy's physical qualities, provided, of course, as in all forms of physical exercise, that it is not overdone, especially at first.

The beginner should go slowly, so as to accustom the muscles to the new exercise. Ten minutes at a time is ample for the first few lessons. Don't exercise too soon after a meal; at least two hours should elapse before wrestling.

In all of the Master-at-Arms tests, Scouts should remember not to lose their tempers. Do nothing underhand or unsportsmanlike. Fair blows or grips never do any harm. They may hurt a little at the time, but it is the mean, unsportsmanlike tricks that sometimes cause permanent injury.

Therefore, in wrestling, don't butt an opponent with the head, pinch or scratch him, or draw the knuckles across his face.

Do not attempt strangles or flying falls. They are quite within the letter of the rules of wrestling, but they are dangerous. An opponent may quite easily be made unconscious with a strangle; and with boys, bones are easily broken with flying falls; that is, throwing an opponent over your head and shoulders.

When you have got your opponent down on both shoulders, don't keep him down needlessly. Spring up at once and help him to rise.

Always choose an opponent about your own weight and strength. If possible, get a good instructor who can teach the various holds, and how to avoid those attempted by your opponent.

The rules of the various styles of wrestling are as follows:

Neither contestant is allowed to rub any oil or grease on his body.

Seconds must not touch their man during a bout. Neither shall they give him advice until a resting period is reached.

Contestants shall be allowed 10 minutes between each bout.

A fall is scored against a man when both shoulders touch the floor at the same time.

A single arm may be pressed against an opponent's throat,

but the free arm or hand must not touch any part of the opponent's head or neck.

The referee shall slap on back or shoulders the wrestler securing a fall, so that the under man will not be strained by being held too long in a possibly painful position.

When wrestlers roll off a mat, under the ropes, or foul the boundary lines in any way, they shall be ordered to the middle of the mat by the referee and to resume the holds they had obtained when moved.

Biting and scratching are fouls.

The timer shall announce when limited time bouts are within three minutes of the end, and then shall call off every minute. He may divide the last minute into halves or quarters if he so desires.

Rolling falls do not count.

The referee shall decide all questions that are not covered by these regulations.

Catch-as-Catch-Can (or Lancashire Style): The catch-as-catch-can style of wrestling is now the most popular branch of the pastime.

Opponents may grasp any part of each other's body.

No form of strangling is permitted, unless especially agreed by the principals.

Before each match, the announcement is usually made, "strangle hold barred".

Instructions for Catch-as-Catch-Can Style: It is difficult to give definite instruction on paper. Practical instruction from a good wrestler is all-important.

Watch your opponent all the time, so that he does not catch you unawares. When down on the mat keep the hands clenched so that your opponent may not be able to catch hold of your fingers and press or twist them. Practise bridging the body. Exercise the muscles of the neck. Practise using the feet and legs, as much as the hands and arms.

Try to conceal your own intentions as much as possible. For instance, suppose you wish to turn your opponent on to, say, his left side, try forcing him to the right and he will do his best to resist this. You have him, therefore, straining in the direction you wish him to go; quickly change your tactics and force him round to the left. This change has to be done like a flash, otherwise your opponent will realise what is intended and will be prepared to meet the new attack.

Græco-Roman (French Style): The Græco-Roman style of wrestling is very similar to the catch-as-catch-can or Lancashire method.

Catching hold of the legs (holds below the waist) is barred.

Tripping constitutes a foul.

The rules of catch-as-catch style that do not conflict with the foregoing regulations may be followed for further guidance.

Cumberland and Westmoreland Wrestling: Contestants take hold and stand chest to chest.

Each man rests his chin on his opponent's shoulder. Each grasps the other round the body. The left arm of each is placed above his opponent's right.

Kicking is barred.

Each man must retain the original hold throughout.

Loosening the hold loses the fall, provided the other man

retains hold.

When a man touches the floor with any part of his body (except his feet, of course) he loses the fall.

When both men fall to the floor, the first one to strike it loses the fall.

"Dog falls" (when both men fall at the same time, so that the referee cannot decide which touches first) are to be wrestled over again.

There is such an infinite variety of wrestling holds and counters that it is quite impossible to give them here. Practise with a good instructor is the only way to learn.

METALWORKER BADGE

A Scout must:

Make and repair some of the simpler tinware articles in common use.

Chip and file small surfaces of cast iron.

Forge wrought iron to hold simple forms, viz., S-hook, ring, staple, hold-fast or pipehook.

Forge and temper a drill or chipping chisel.

Fit and braze two pieces of wrought iron together.

Explain the names, uses and construction of metalwork tools and apparatus in common use, and give reasons for shapes, cutting angles, etc., of tools.

Explain the composition and properties of solders, fluxes and metals.

Be familiar with ordinary workshop practices and processes.

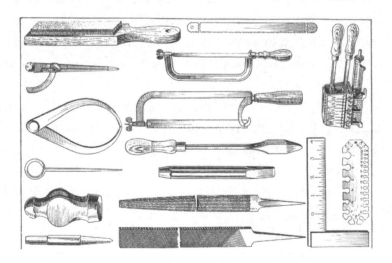

METALWORKER'S TOOLS

MINER BADGE

A Scout must have a general knowledge of one particular branch of the mining industry, such as coal, iron or other mineral, with the special dangers involved, and safeguards against them, and must have worked below the surface for not less than six months.

"Volunteers for rescue work!" When the call was made at the Cadeby Colliery disaster of 1912, one of the first to be on the spot was Scoutmaster Prince. He joined the party of rescuers on their perilous errand and went to his death. The Cadeby pit is his grave. At the same disaster, one of Mr Prince's Scouts also perished. Scout Smith was found dead by the side of his pony, which he had evidently been trying to save. Scouting has taken a strong hold in many colliery districts, and if it can produce men and boys prepared to act in every emergency as these two heroic examples, it has indeed a place in the colliery as everywhere else.

To attempt within limited space to give anything like adequate information regarding mining work is impossible, and only a very general survey will be attempted. As in many other things, "an ounce of practice is worth a pound of theory", and more will be learned in connection with the miner's badge during the six months' practice than will be gleaned from a study of the following remarks. They may, however, serve as a suitable introduction to the practical work.

To begin with, let us consider in what manner the mineral is taken from its bed, and the methods employed in cutting it below grounds.

Methods of Mining

There are two principal methods of mining used according as it is desired to support the stratum above the mineral bed or to allow it to fall. The first is known as the Pillar and Stall system. In order to operate in this system, "places" are driven in the untouched coal, so that the area of coal to be worked is divided into large rectangular pillars by the means of the narrow places called "stalls". Thereafter, the pillars of coal are extracted, the timber used to support the roof is withdrawn and the roof falling in fills up the space caused by the extraction of the coal. This method is best used for thick seams of coal. The most dangerous part of this work is in extracting the pillars. It is well to get the coal out as quickly as possible, and yet too many pillars must not be removed at once. As soon as a solid portion of coal has been driven through, it should be extracted as quickly as possible, for the coal in pillars deteriorates when left standing for long. In extracting the pillars, the coal should be taken from each side simultaneously.

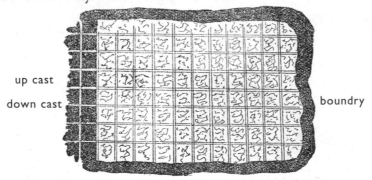

up cast

down cast   boundry

Pillars marked thus 🔲 have been taken
on retreating from boundry
PILLAR AND STALL.

The other method used for the extraction of minerals is called the Longwall system, which aims at the extraction of the contents of the bed in one operation. There are two varieties of this system, one called the Longwall advancing, and the other the Longwall retreating. In the first of these, the whole of the coal is worked out from the shaft to the boundaries, the miners cutting the coal while advancing from the shaft. No effort is made to support the roof beyond what is necessary for the protection of the men. The other variation is for places to be driven to the boundaries and then for the coal to be worked backwards towards the shaft. This latter method is generally considered a safer system, as the roof pressure is supported by the solid coal while the miners work towards the shaft. There is no danger of any section of the mine collapsing. Ventilation is easier with the Longwall system, which is generally the best where there are thin seams to be worked. For thick seams, however, where there is little rubbish to be had for packs in the wall, it is unsuitable.

There seems to be little difference between the Longwall and the Pillar and Stall methods of mining with regards to safety. As many falls of roof endangering life take place under the one system as the other.

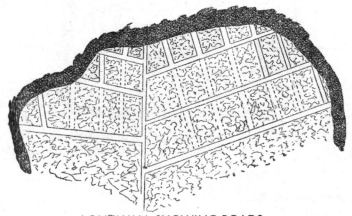

LONGWALL SHOWING ROADS.

MISSIONER BADGE

The qualifications are:

A general elementary knowledge of sick-nursing; invalid cookery, sickroom attendance, bed-making, and ventilation.

Ability to help aged and infirm.

In case of illness, the first thing the Missioner may be called on to do is to prepare the room for the patient. If it is possible to select the room, one should be selected which has a southerly or southwesterly exposure, in order that the patient may have as much sunshine as possible. It is also essential that there should be a fireplace in the room, both on account of heat and of ventilation.

In selecting a room for anyone suffering from an infectious disease, the following points should be noted:

The room should be as far away as possible from other bedrooms, living rooms and kitchen; it should be near water, to save much carrying; it should be convenient for the emptying of slops, in order to prevent carrying such infected matter through the house.

In preparing a room for an infectious case, all heavy curtains, stuffed chairs and unnecessary furniture and ornaments should be removed; also any drapery round the bed. If there is time to let it thoroughly dry, the floor should be washed with 5 per cent carbolic but, if there is not time for it to dry, it should be merely rubbed over with a damp cloth.

Once the patient is in the room, the following points have to be considered:

Temperature of the Room: The temperature of the room is noted by means of a thermometer which should be hung behind the bed about the same level as the patient's head.

As a general rule the room should be kept at about 65° Fahrenheit, but, in cases of fever, 60°F is high enough, and on the other hand in lung and chest troubles, the temperature should be about 70°F. Should the room become too warm the window should be opened wider, and the fire allowed to get lower; should the room become too cold, the window may be partially closed, and the fire made bigger, also the patient should be kept well covered. Under no circumstances should the gas be lit to heat the room, as this uses up much valuable oxygen from the air.

Ventilation consists in keeping the air in the room fresh. This is most important in the sickroom, because an invalid requires fresh air to help his recovery, and because in illness the body gives off a large number of impurities. The windows should be kept open from the top, but care should be taken that the bed is not placed between the door and the window. An open chimney, with a coal fire burning, not only keeps the room cheery, but also is a good means of ventilating the room as it causes an updraught. If there is too much air near the bed, place a screen between it and the window, but do not shut the window. If a screen is not available, improvise one by throwing a blanket or rug over a clotheshorse or over a cord fastened to two convenient points.

Airing a room consists in completely changing the air that is in the room, and, where a patient is confined to one room for a considerable time, this is very necessary. The best way to air a room is first to cover the patient well, then to open the windows top and bottom and also to open the door. If there is any fear of the draught striking the patient, a draught-screen may be placed between him and the open window.

Body Temperature: The normal temperature of the body is 98.4° Fahrenheit. If the temperature rises more than a degree above this, the patient is said to be feverish. Anyone whose temperature is 100°F or over should be kept in bed and the doctor sent for, and if a feverish patient's temperature should rise still further the doctor should be informed at once. The patient's temperature is usually taken twice a day – in the morning and in the evening – and it is generally found to be slightly higher in the evening.

Fever is not a disease, but a symptom common to many diseases and illnesses.

In addition to a rise in temperature, the patient's pulse will be quickened, and the skin will be hot and dry.

How to Change the Bedclothes: To change the under sheet, roll it lengthwise; that is, begin at the side. Push soiled sheet and all coverings towards the patient, leaving the mattress bare. On this, lay the clean roll, tucking one side under the mattress, unroll it towards the patient, and move him over the roll on the smooth space, keeping him covered with the top blanket. Go to the other side of the bed, pull out underblanket and soiled sheet, finish unrolling clean sheet and tuck it in. Lay the clean upper sheet over the top blanket and cover it with another blanket. When these are in place, remove the blankets that are next to the patient, and he will be left lying between clean sheets, without having been exposed for an instant to the chance of taking cold.

Bed Sores are due to the death of the skin at a point exposed to prolonged pressure during a patient's confinement to bed, when, owing to infirmity or a fractured bone, he is compelled to lie in one position without moving. Bed sores are preventable by careful nursing.

In cases of severe fracture, damage to the spine etc., it may be necessary to get a waterbed. To fill the waterbed, place it empty under the patient, and then pour in water at a temperature of 70°F. Do not overfill the bed, but have it so that if one hand is placed above the bed, and the other below it, the two hands just fail to touch.

Giving of Medicine: Never give a patient medicine without the doctor's orders.

Never give a person anyone else's medicine.

Look at the label every time before administering medicine.

Find out if the medicine is to be given before or after meals.

Use a graduated measuring glass as spoons vary in size.

If you miss giving the patient a dose of medicine, don't double the next dose.

If a patient is asleep when his medicine should be given, do not waken him, unless the doctor has told you to do so, or unless you know that it is important and that the patient will go to sleep at once again. Do not be like the nurse who wakened the patient to give him a sleeping draught.

Disinfectants: The natural disinfectants are – pure air and sunshine. Water usually contains germs which may be morbid in their action or not; but, if the water is boiled, the vitality of the germs is thereby destroyed, and it is thus rendered aseptic.

There is a very common and very bad method often used in a sickroom, that is using what are termed deodorants when there is an offensive smell caused by illness. The deodorants simply make a stronger odour, which prevents one noticing the previous offensive odour. They don't drive away the offensive odour, which still remains, and which could be easily driven away by sufficient ventilation, as already explained.

Always wash your hands in a disinfectant when you leave the sick-room, and all dishes should be disinfected before being returned to the kitchen; such dishes should not be mixed with those in regular use. The nurse should have lots of fresh air, and should go for an hour's walk each day.

Diet: The diet will be carefully laid down by the doctor, and his instructions in this respect should be carefully adhered to. If a patient is put on a light diet, this means that meat is not allowed. It includes beef tea, barley water, gruel, arrowroot, etc., and generally also fish or fowl occasionally. A milk diet includes milk, arrowroot, sago, tapioca, rice etc. There are a number of prepared invalid foods to be had, along with which full instructions as to cooking them are given. In addition, a Scout might be called on to prepare some of the foods which are in constant use in a sickroom, such as:

Beef Tea: When ordering the beef, state that it is wanted to make beef tea. Cut the beef up finely, remove the skin and fat, put it into a clean pot with its own weight of water, then put the lid on. Allow it to soak for an hour. Place the pot on the hob for two to three hours – but never let it actually boil – then place in an oven for four hours or so. Allow it to cool, then, when cold, skim off the fat. Heat up when required, but do not boil.

Gruel: Put two tablespoonfuls of oatmeal in a saucepan, add a little water, and thoroughly mix. Add a pint of milk or water and boil gently for 30 minutes, stirring it constantly. Put in salt according to taste.

Barley Water: (This is a most refreshing drink). First, wash the barley well in cold water. Put two ounces into a jug, add a little sugar, and pour on a pint of boiling water. Let it cool, and strain before using. The taste is improved by putting in the outer peel of a lemon before pouring on the water (about a quarter of a whole lemon peel is sufficient).

General Notes for the Sick Room: Keep the pillow well under the shoulders; nothing is more tiresome to a weak person than to have the edge come just in the hollow of the neck, throwing the chin forward on the breast. Gently comb and brush the hair, and if there is a beard keep it washed and free from tangles. If the patient is a woman, part the back hair and braid each portion. It may be coiled high on the head or allowed to hang in two tails. The nails on both hands and feet should be carefully attended to.

If the carpet cannot be removed, sweep it daily with a carpet sweeper or a broom with a cloth wrapped round it, and burn the dust. Wipe the woodwork and furniture daily with a damp cloth. Never leave milk standing in a sickroom; it quickly absorbs impurities. If obliged to wait a few moments until the invalid is ready to take it, cover the glass containing it. Make it a rule to leave nothing in the sickroom that is not positively needed there. Remove every cup, glass and spoon as soon as used, and wash all bottles when empty. Keep the little table beside the bed covered with a white cloth, and see that it is always spotless. Be as cheerful as possible, and try to leave worries on the other side of the door.

Creaking doors and squeaky shoes irritate the patient.

Do not have the sun shining directly into the patient's eyes if it can be avoided.

Last of all, remember to put your Missioner's knowledge into practice when there is anyone in your own home suffering from illness or even minor ailments.

MUSICIAN BADGE

A Scout must be able to play a musical instrument correctly other than triangle, and to read simple piano music. Or to play properly any kind of musical toy, such as a penny whistle, mouth organ, etc., and sing a song.

No written instruction can be given for this badge. The Scout must work up the music on the selected instrument.

It should, however, be noted that to "read simple music," means ability to play a simple piece of music, given by the examiner, which the Scout has not previously seen or practised.

BOY PLAYING A CORNET

NATURALIST BADGE

A Scout must make a collection of the leaves of thirty different trees or of sixty species of wild flower, ferns or grasses, dried and mounted in a book and correctly named.

Or, alternatively, he must make coloured drawings of twenty flowers, ferns or grasses from life, or twelve sketches from life of animals and birds. Original sketches, as well as the finished pictures, to be submitted.

Or, alternatively he must be able to name sixty different kinds of animals, insects, reptiles or birds in a museum or zoological garden, or from unnamed coloured plates, and give particulars of the lives, habits, appearance, and markings of twenty of them.

Or, alternatively, he must describe the habits, and recognise by their songs, calls or voices, 30 different kinds of birds or animals.

This is a comparatively easy badge, because a Scout has the opportunity of picking one out of three alternatives.

There is nothing to explain in this badge, as the veriest tenderfoot will understand what is required and how to set about passing the test.

Questions have been asked as to whether in the test for the Naturalist's Badge candidates should invariably make their drawings from life. The Committee was of the opinion that the intention of the test was clear, but determined that as the wording left room for doubt, the necessary alterations be made in the next issue of the Regulations to the effect that all drawings have to be made from life.

OARSMAN BADGE

A Scout must be able to manage a boat singlehanded, row and skull, and be able to punt (in rivers) or skull over the stern or paddle a canoe; be able to steer a boat under oars and bring her alongside a vessel and landing-stage; must be able to tow and be towed, and secure a boat to a buoy or alongside a wharf.

To manage a boat singlehanded: See that you sit as near amidships as possible so that the boat is in proper trim and therefore easily managed. Try to get some mark astern so as to ensure making a good course, and glance frequently over the shoulder, so as to keep clear of other boats or obstructions.

In sculling over the stern: ensure a good foothold, hold the loom of the oar well up, and keep only the blade submerged; otherwise it is an easy matter to "catch a crab" or even find yourself over the side. Twist the oar in a sort of figure-of-eight manner to propel the boat, and to steer pull more strongly one way than the other. Again, practice is necessary to become expert.

Punting by means of a pole: Is more difficult than the two previous methods of propelling a craft and in which great care is necessary. Place the pole down in a vertical manner close alongside your craft and, when the pole is leaning aft, push fairly hard. Do not allow the push to be too long before you recover for the next move.

Should the paint pole become fixed in the bottom, great care must be observed because your craft is getting further from the position all the time and you may be pulled over the side.

Paddling a canoe: Sit in the bottom of the canoe facing the way the canoe is travelling. With a double-bladed paddle each blade is dipped alternately in the water slightly forward of your position. With a single-bladed paddle you can keep the canoe going straight by pulling hard and then feathering the blade or turning it slightly outwards from the side. Or again, by changing the position of the paddle to the opposite side of the canoe.

To bring a boat alongside a vessel or landing stage: In all cases, should there be any tide, it is prudent to come alongside head to tide. On approaching and when about 20 yards or so from the wharf or vessel, give the order "Bows" when the bow oar will "toss his oar" and "boat it" and stand by with his boathook ready to fend off or get hold. When you consider you have sufficient way to reach your objective, give the order "Way enough" and the crew will "toss their oars" and "boat them".

Towing and being towed: When towing another boat, make a bowline in her painter and secure it by passing it up between the two after thwarts and reeving a stretcher through it to act as a toggle. When being towed astern of another boat the closer the better. If a number of boats are being towed, the largest and heaviest should be the foremost in the line; they can be secured by passing a hawser astern to which each boat is secured by hitching her bow and stern painters to it with a rolling hitch.

PATHFINDER BADGE

A Scout must:

Know every lane, bye-path, and short cut for a distance of at least two miles in every direction around the local Scouts' headquarters in the country or for one mile if in a town, and to have a general knowledge of the district within a five-mile radius of his local headquarters, so as to be able to guide people at any time, by day or night.

Know the general direction of the principal neighbouring towns for a distance of twenty-five miles, and be able to give strangers clear directions how to get to them.

In the country, in a two-mile radius, know the names of the different farms, their approximate acreage and stock; or, in a town, in a half-mile radius, know the principal livery stables, corn chandlers, forage merchants, bakers and butchers.

In town or country, know where are the police stations, hospitals, doctors, telegraph, telephone offices, fire engines, turncocks, blacksmiths, job-masters and factories where over a dozen horses are kept.

Know something of the history of the place, or of any old buildings, such as the church or castle.

As much as possible of the above information should be entered on a large-scale map for permanent reference at the local headquarters.

In towns where there are undesirable streets or localities, Associations may, with the consent of the Commissioner, vary the half-mile radius round the local Scouts' Headquarters, so as to exclude such undesirable localities.

For this badge, a Scout requires to be efficient in map-reading and map-drawing. Book instruction is otherwise not required. The Scout must walk about the district and note the points required.

He should also carefully study a 6-inch ordnance map and also a 1-inch map of the country within the radius.

PHOTOGRAPHER BADGE

A Scout must have a knowledge of the theory and use of lenses, and the construction of cameras, action of developers. He must take, develop, and print twelve separate subjects – three interiors, three portraits, three landscapes and three instantaneous "action" photos.

Lenses: So far as possible, we shall endeavour to avoid technical terms, but at the same time try to explain the meaning of the special terms used with reference to lenses.

To fully understand the working of a photographic lens, it is first necessary to understand something of the action of light.

Any object which can be seen, is sending off rays of light in every direction, from every point, no matter whether the rays come from the object's own illumination or from reflected light.

Let us take a piece of cardboard and make a very small hole in it at, and assume that this hole is only capable of admitting one ray of light. Then place an object in front of it. As the point is sending off rays in every possible direction, and as the hole at can only admit one ray, one and only one can pass through, all others are stopped by the cardboard. The ray that passes through, proceeds till it is stopped by a screen, plate or film, and forms a little point of light. Photographs can be made with a small hole of this kind (this is called pin-hole photography), but it is difficult to make the hole small enough to give sufficient definition, and the exposure requires to be very long. To avoid these defects and difficulties, a lens is used.

Interiors mean the inside of churches, houses, or any building.

"Action" Photos mean a moving object, such as a horse jumping, a moving train, or a boy running, etc.

This badge should present no difficulties to regular amateur photographers, but those who are just taking up the art should not go in for the badge until they have had a few months practical experience; and to them, I say that very little can be learned from a book – the best thing they can do is to have a friend who has had previous experience with them, from the buying of the camera and apparatus to the developing and final printing of their first negative.

As regards the camera itself, cameras may be said to belong to, roughly, three kinds: (1) the Magazine or Box-shaped Camera; (2) the Hand or Stand Camera, with either a plate-box or dark slides; (3) the "Kodak" or other form of folding pocket camera.

Your camera being loaded, you now proceed to choose good objects to take for your badge. You will first find the general processes which apply to the four classes of subject, and the special points to be noted in each class, viz., portraits, landscapes, interiors, snapshots.

Having chosen your subject, the first thing to do is to get the aperture (or size of opening) you want in the diaphragm, remembering that while a small aperture gives a clearer photo, a much longer exposure is necessary than with a large aperture. If the light is dull and diffused, it will probably be necessary to keep the aperture open wide at F8. Only use F32 when there is strong sunlight.

The next step is to focus your camera (that is, always supposing it is one which can be focussed), if the distances are marked at the side of the ratchet.

Better still is to use a focussing screen, moving the lens in its frame back and forward till you get a clear image on the ground glass. Then remove the focussing screen and (seeing that the cap is on, if you do not have a time and instantaneous shutter), pull back the cover of the slide, leaving the plate ready to be exposed.

And now is the most difficult part: to know how long you should expose the plate. This can only be learned by experience and experiment, since your exposure must vary according to the make and speed of plate you used, the stop (or aperture), the amount of light, your lens and the subject you are taking.

Developing: There are many made-up developers to be had from photographic dealers, but if a Scout wishes to understand the subject fully, he should make up his own developer.

As to exactly what developer to choose it is difficult to advise, as each one has a special qualification of its own, and different makers' plates may require different treatment. Of course, any one of the many developers will produce a satisfactory negative from any plate, provided the exposure has been correct; but delicate graduation of tone in landscapes etc. are produced in different plates by different means.

No general rules can be laid down as to when to stop the process of development. With some brands of plates, very little of the image should appear at the back of the plate; while with others, most of the image must be distinctly visible.

Experience is the only way to learn, and it is best to keep to one brand of plates until their working is thoroughly known.

When development is completed, the developer should be poured off and the plate well rinsed under a tap or in one or two changes of water. The plate is then ready for fixing. After development is finished, the reduced silver that forms the image remains mixed with a quantity of yellowish unaltered silver bromide. If this is not removed it would not be possible to print from the negative, and the silver bromide would gradually darken when exposed to light.

This unaltered silver bromide has to be dissolved out, and this process is called "fixing". The plate is immersed in a solution of sodium thiosulphate (formerly called sodium hyposulphite), commonly called "hypo". The strength should be one part hypo to four parts water. Hypo cools the water considerably while dissolving, so that the bath should be mixed in tepid water an hour or two before required.

Finally, the plate has to be washed, and this is best done in a washing-tank, which keeps the plates from touching each other, and, by keeping the plates upright, allows the chemicals to be carried off. The plates should be rinsed in several changes of water and then placed in the washing-tank and left in running water (and the water must cover them completely) for at least two hours, and, if possible, they should be left to wash over night; a little alum in the water will prevent the edges "frilling".

After being washed, the plates should be lifted out of the tank in the "rock" (the inside part of the tank), and left to thoroughly dry before the printing is commenced.

Films can be washed by putting them into the water loose – that is, without using the washing-tank – and are dried by being pinned up.

Printing: Printing can be done on either Daylight or Gaslight Sensitised Paper.

PILOT BADGE

A Scout must be able to sail a boat, tack, wear, reef, make and shorten sail. He must have full knowledge of the Admiralty chart for the nearest port and the coast on each side of it. He must know the buoys, beacons, landmarks and leading marks into and out of the harbour and be able to heave the lead. He must know the rule of the Road at Sea, the lights carried by all classes of vessels, the danger and storm signals and the mercantile code of signals. He must be able to fix positions by means of cross bearings, both from land and sea, and must keep a log for at least a month, registering the wind, weather, barometer and thermometer, as generally carried out at sea.

The knowledge that an aspirant for the Pilot's Badge is required to possess covers a large ground and really means that he must be a competent amateur sailor both in theory and practice.

It will specially appeal to the Boy Scout who has been brought up in a seaside port, who is constantly being brought into touch with seafaring men and who, therefore, has the necessary facilities for supplementing theoretical instruction by personal experience, and opportunities of frequently sailing in the adjacent waters under the guidance and tuition of a friendly salt.

Much may be thoroughly learned at home by the fireside or in the garden, and it is with these subjects that we shall deal first.

The Chart

A chart is simply a map of the coastline and adjacent sea prepared by the Admiralty after the most careful and scrupulous survey.

It gives the minutest details of the coast itself and outlying dangers, and the different depth of water all over the sea is stated by small figures which indicate in feet or fathoms the depth at these places at one uniform time, low water ordinary spring tides.

The following little chart giving an outline of the Coast of Spain, but no details, will illustrate the meaning of such terms as latitude, longitude.

Mercator's Chart

Charts generally have a compass printed on them, with an arrow to represent the North point; the top being the NORTH part of the chart, the bottom SOUTH, the right-hand side EAST, and the left-hand side WEST. Meridians are the lines running North and South on the chart; those on the sides, which are divided into degrees and miles, are called Graduated Meridians. Parallels of latitude are the lines running East and West; those at the top and bottom are divided into degrees and miles, and are called Graduated Parallels. Latitude is measured at the sides on the Graduated Meridians. Longitude is measured at the top and bottom on the Graduated Parallels.

Scale 1 inch — Latitude 40° to 44° N.
Longitude 8° to 12° W.

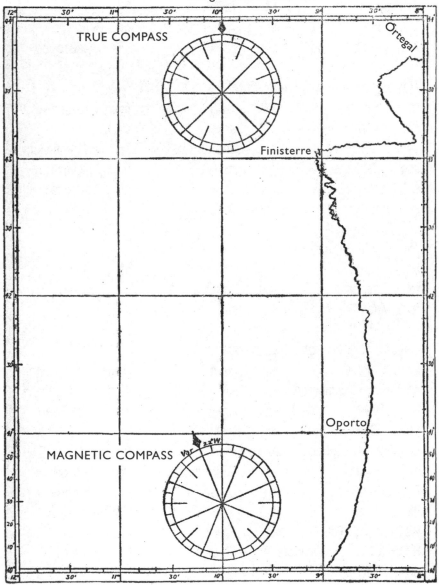

Chart Abbreviations

Relating to Colour:

d......blue	blk......black	br......brown
d......dark	gn......green	gy......grey
w......white	y......yellow	spk......speckled

Relating to Substance of Bottom:

cl......clay	m.......mud	oys......oysters
crl......coral	r.......rock	mrl.......marl
peb.......pebbles	s......sand	for......foraminifera
shg......shingle	g......gravel	gl......globigerina
sh......shells	oz......ooze	pt......pteropod
st......stones	wd......weed	rad......radiolaria

Relating to Nature of Bottom:

brk......broken	stf......stiff	sft......soft
rot......rotten	grd......ground	c......coarse
f......fine	h......hard	

General Abbreviations used on Charts:

Alt......Altitude	Kn......Knot	Magz......Magazine
Anchge......Anchorage	G......Gulf	Magc......Magnetic
B......Bay	Gt......Great	Mt......Mountain
Bk......Bank	H......Hour	
ObsnSpot + ... Observation Spot		Bn......Beacon
Hd......Head	Bar......Barometer	Ho......House
P......Port	Baty......Battery	Hr......Harbour
Pk......Peak	C......Cape	H.W. ....High
Water Pt......Point	Cr......Creek	
H.W.F. & C. ......High Water Full & Change		R...... River
Ch......Church	Rf......Reef	
C.G. ...... Coastguard	Rk......Rock	Cath......Cathedral
I......Island	Sh......Shoal	Chan......Channel
Is.......Islands	Sp...... Springs	Cold......Coloured

L......Lake   Sd......Sound
E.D. ......A rock or shoal reported whose existence is doubtful
L.B. ......Life Boat   Stn...... Station L.W. ...... Low Water
Stt ...... Strait   Lt...... Light   Tel......TelegraphL.
S.S. ...... Life Saving Station   Therm ...... Thermometer
Vil......Village   Ft......Feet   Lat......Latitude
Varn......Variations   F.S.......Flag Staff
Long......Longitude   W.Pl. ...... Watering Place
Fms......Fathoms   Np......Neaps
P.D....... A danger is known to exist, but its position is doubtful

Abbreviations used to denote Colour of Buoys:

B	placed near a buoy	Black
Cheq	"	Chequered
H S	"	Horizonal Stripes
R	"	Red
V S	" -	Vertical Stripes
W	"	White

Sounding Lines

Fathom Lines

Single Dots thus, ...	=	1
Dots in pairs thus, ...	=	2
Dots in threes thus, ...	=	3
Dots in fours thus, ...	=	4
Dots in fives thus, ...	=	5
Dots in sixes thus, ...	=	6
Lines and dots thus, ___ . ____.____.____.____.	=	7
Lines and pairs of dots thus, ____ .. ____ .. ____ .. ____ .. =		8
Lines and threes of dots thus, ____ ... ____ ... ____ ... ____ ...	=	9
Continuous dots thus, ...	=	10

Hydrographic Chart Conventional Signs

Trees

Cultivated Land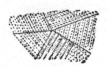

Swampy, Marshy, or Mossy Land

Sand Hills or Dunes

Cliffy Coast Line

Steep coast

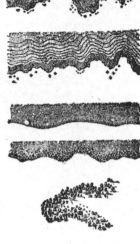

Sandy Shore

Stony or Shingly Shore

Mangroves

Figures bracketed against islands
and rocks express the Heights in
Feet above High Water,
Ordinary Springs, or above the sea
in cases where there is no tide

Towns, Villages, or Houses

Villages or Houses

Roads
Track or Footpath
Railway
Tramway

Churches or Chapels

Temples

Windmill

Triangulation Station
    Beacon, Chimney, Flagstaff or
    other fixed points

Lights, Position of

Rocky Ledges and isolated rocks,
dry at Low Water Springs

Sandy Beach and Banks,
dry at Low Water Springs

Stones, Shingle or Gravel,
dry at Low Water Springs

Mud Banks, dry at Low
Water Springs

Sand and Gravel or Stones,
dry at Low Water Springs

Sand and Mud,
dry at Low Water Springs

Coral Reefs

Rock awash at Low Water Springs

Rock with less than 6 feet of water over
it at Low Water Springs. On small scale
charts, this symbol is used for rocks
with greater depths of water over them.

Rocks with limiting danger line

Rock or Shoal, the position of which
is doubtful

Reported Rock or Shoal, the existence
of which is doubtful

Breakers along a shore

Overfalls and Tide Rips

Eddies

Kelp

Anchorage for large vessels

Anchorage for small vessels

Light buoys

Bell Buoys

Buoys with Topmarks

Spar Buoys

Mooring Buoys

Light Vessels or Floats

Aids to Memory in Four Verses

BY THOMAS GRAY.

I. *Two Steamships Meeting*
  When both Lights you see ahead,
  Port your Helm and show your Red.

II. *Two Steamships Passing*
  Green to Green – or Red to Red –
  Perfect Safety – go ahead.

III. *Two Steamships Crossing*
Note: This is the position of greatest danger – there is nothing
for it but a good look-out, caution and judgement.

If to your Starboard Red appear
It is your duty to keep clear;
To act as judgment says is proper
To Port – or Starboard – Back – or stop her.

But when upon your Port is seen
A Steamer Starboard Light of Green,
There's not so much for you to do,
For Green to Port keeps clear of you.

IV. *All Ships must keep a look-out and Steamships must Stop and go astern if necessary*
Both in safety and in doubt
Always keep a good look-out;
In danger with no room to turn,
Ease her – Stop her – go Astern.

V. *Every Vessel overtaking any other shall keep out of the way of the overtaken Vessel*

Sound Signals for Fog etc.

Steam Whistle or Siren: One prolonged blast at intervals of not more than 2 minutes.

Two prolonged blasts at intervals of not more than 2 minutes, with an interval of about 1 second duration between them.

Three blasts, one prolonged, followed by two short blasts at intervals of not more than 2 minutes.

Steam vessel having way upon her.

Steam vessel under way, but stopped and having no way

upon her.

Vessel when towing – vessels employed laying down or picking up telegraph cable – vessel not under command – vessel towed (optional).

Fog Horn: One blast at intervals of not more than 1 minute.

Two blasts in succession, at intervals of not more than 1 minute.

Three blasts in succession, at intervals of not more than 1 minute.

Sailing vessel under way on starboard tack.

Sailing vessel under way on port tack.

Sailing vessel under way with wind abaft the beam.

Bell: A bell rung rapidly for about 5 seconds, at intervals of not more than 1 minute.

Vessel at anchor.

Heaving the Lead

The apparatus known as the lead and lead-line merely consists of 7 lbs of lead, shaped as shown in the accompanying diagram with about 25 fathoms of line attached to it.

It is used for ascertaining the depth of water and is marked as follows:

To fit and mark a lead-line, proceed as follows: After having well stretched the line, splice in one end an eye about 8 inches in length, and wet the line. All the marks you put in the line must be tucked in twice through the strands of the line, and each mark should be about 3 inches in length.

Marks

At 2 fathoms	-	A piece of leather with two ends.
" 3 "	-	A piece of leather with three ends.
" 5 "	-	A piece of white calico.
" 7 "	-	A piece of red bunting.
" 10 "	-	Leather with hole in it.
" 13 "	-	A piece of blue cloth.
" 15 "	-	A piece of white calico.
" 17 "	-	A piece of red bunting.
" 20 "	-	A piece of whipcord with two knots.

SOUNDING
LEAD

Unmarked fathoms 4, 6 etc., are termed deeps.

Note: The reason for using calico, cloth and bunting, is that the difference my be felt when too dark to see, and the marks thus recognised.

If the vessel is stationary, obviously all that need be done is to lower the lead into the water until it touches the bottom, when, of course, the depth will be indicated by the water line.

The operation known as heaving the lead is one that requires some skill and much practice. The vessel being under way, the leadsman stands on a little grating platform projecting from the side of the vessel, technically known as the "chains", with a broad canvas belt around his waist secured to the ship so that he can lean well over, and then, with the coil in his left hand, and the lead with a couple of fathoms of line hanging from his right hand, he gives it a few preliminary swings to and fro and then swings it twice completely round his head, finally launching it as far ahead as possible, so that the lead has time to sink and reach the bottom before the vessel's speed brings him vertically over it.

Then, by rapidly gathering in the slack link he recognises that the lead is touching the bottom by tapping the ground smartly and calculating the depth by the nearest mark to the water line, and reports the sounding.

If it is 5 fathoms, he calls out, "By the mark 5." If it is 4 fathoms, he calls out, "By the deep 4," and so on.

The correct method of reporting intermediate fractions of a fathom is somewhat curious and is the result of long established custom. For 7½ fathoms, he calls out, "And a half seven." For 6¾ fathoms, he calls out, "A quarter less seven." For 6¼ fathoms, he calls out, "And a quarter six," and so on, all quarter, halves and three-quarter fathoms being strictly reported in this manner.

A good leadsman is not made in a day, incessant practice being required.

With a vessel going 6 knots, depths up to 8 fathoms can be got by a smart leadsman with a 7 lb lead, but, above that speed, a 14 lb lead should be used.

Keeping a Log

This means keeping a daily record of the weather, and, if at sea, an account of the courses steered with the distances run and observations taken for fixing a ship's position.

As far as the Boy Scout is concerned, however, the logbook will be purely a meteorological one that he can rule out for himself in an ordinary exercise book.

In the keeping of the logbook abbreviations may be used, the direction of the wind should be recorded to the nearest point and its force may be indicated by the Beaufort Scale, which is here given:

0 = Calm	7 = Moderate gale
1 = Light air	8 = Fresh gale
2 = Light breeze	9 = Strong gale
3 = Gentle breeze	10 = Whole gale
4 = Moderate breeze	11 = Storm
5 = Fresh breeze	12 = Hurricane
6 = Strong breeze	

In entering the state of the weather, the following codes may be employed, the underlining of the letter to imply the prefix "heavy".

b = Blue sky	p = Passing showers
c = Clouds (detached)	q = Squally
d = Drizzling rain	r = Rain
f = Fog	s = Snow
g = Gloomy	t = Thunder
h = Hail	u = Ugly (threatening appearances)
l = Lightning	v = Visibility (objects at a distance very clear)
m = Misty (hazy)	o = Overcast w = Dew

The state of the sea may also be indicated by numerals:

0 = Calm	5 = Rather rough
1 = Very smooth	6 = Rough
2 = Smooth	7 = High
3 = Slight	8 = Very high
4 = Moderate	9 = Tremendous

SAMPLE OF PAGE IN LOG BOOK.

Date……………..   Name of Recorder…………………………….

Time	Wind	Force	Sea	Time of H.W.	W'ther	Clouds	Bar	Ther.
4 a.m.	N.N.W.	7	5	-	g	Cumulus	29.26"	50°F.
8 a.m.	"	7	5	8.20 a.m.	g	"	29.38	58
Noon	N.W.	8	6	-	d	Overcast	29.3	68
4 p.m.	"	8	6	-	r	"	29.3	62
8 p.m.	"	9	7	8.42 p.m.	o	"	29.25	60
Midnight	"	8	7	-	o	"	29.25	48

Weather Hints

There are some old doggerel weather rhymes that are not to
be despised.

> A red sky in the morning
> Is the sailor's warning,
> A red sky at night
> Is the sailor's delight.

In squalls:

> When the rain's before the wind
> Topsail halliards you must mind,
> When the wind's before the rain
> Soon you may make sail again.

> At sea with low and falling glass
> Soundly sleeps the careless ass,
> Only when it's high and rising
> Safely rests the careful wise 'un.

Mackerel sky and mare's tails
Make lofty ships carry low sails.

The wind will blow hard when the gull comes ashore.

Sea-gull, sea-gull, sit on the sand
It's never good weather when you're on the land.

Hard-edged oily- (or greasy-) looking clouds tell of wind; soft-looking clouds fine weather.

High upper clouds crossing the sun or moon, in an opposite direction to the wind blowing, foretell a change in its direction.

A high dawn – that is, when the first streaks of light appear over a bank of clouds instead of near the horizon, foretells wind.

A low dawn – fine weather.

On our own coasts the light mare's-tail or brush-head cloud (cirrus), moving from N.W. on a fine day, is an almost infallible sign of the approach of a depression or storm system.

This forementioned cirrus, when seen lying at rest in faint cross lines, is a good sign of settled weather. A mackerel sky moving fast from the westward or long feathers of cirrus radiating from the west, as is sometimes seen at sunset, are both signs of an approaching westerly gale.

PIONEER BADGE

A Scout must have extra efficiency in pioneering in the following tests, or suitable equivalents:

Fell a 9-inch tree or scaffolding pole neatly and quickly.

Tie eight kinds of knots quickly in the dark or blindfolded.

Lash spars properly together for scaffolding.

Build a model bridge or derrick.

Make a camp kitchen.

Build a hut of one kind or another suitable for three occupants.

There are two styles of lashing, called square lashing and diagonal lashing.

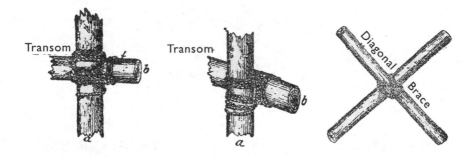

Square lashing: The "square lashing" is used when two spars are to be lashed together at right angles (or nearly so), such as a horizontal to a perpendicular spar, or transverse to longitudinal. In the latter case the lashing may be commenced on either, but in the former case it should commence on the upright spar below the position for the horizontal one. A clove hitch is first made round the upright, and the end of the rope twisted round the standing part of the lashing to stow it away. The lashing now proceeds round the back of the horizontal spar; round the face of the upright spar, above; round the back of the horizontal spar, on the opposite side from first turn; then round the face of the upright spar, thus reaching the place from which it started. At least four of these turns should be taken in succession, keeping them inside on one spar, and outside on the other, never allowing them to over-ride. Two or more frapping turns are now made between the spars, and well beaten in, so as to tighten up all the turns of the lashing. Two half-hitchs (or a clove hitch) are made on the most convenient spar to secure the end of the lashing, any portion of the rope being left neatly stowed away.

An Earth Anchorage is a log or logs of timber buried in the ground at sufficient depth to resist the strain of cables, guys etc., which may be made fast thereto.

EARTH ANCHORAGE

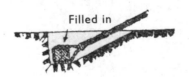

Filled in

Holdfasts (furnish a means for securing the ends of ropes to the ground. They are constructed with pickets driven unto the ground securely, in sufficient numbers, and at proper angles, to suit the strain, which will ultimately come upon them. Where the strain may be great an arrangement of three stout pickets, driven one behind the other, a short distance apart, and in the line of the expected strain, should be adopted. The head of the front picket should be secured by a lashing to the foot of the next.

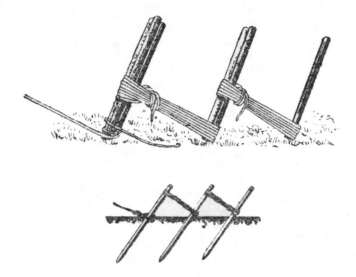

The lashing is then twisted tightly by means of a small stake inserted between the turns, the point of the stake being finally driven into the ground to maintain the tautness of the lashing. When the second and third pickets have been similarly treated, the "holdfast" is ready, and any strain that may come on the front picket will be distributed to the other two. With heavy strains, the "holdfast" may be formed, having a cluster of three for the front, two in the second and one in the third positions.

Bridges: There are several forms of bridges, varying according to the materials available, the kind of traffic for which the bridge will be used, and the breadth, depth etc. of the span to be bridged over.

When the bottom can be touched throughout, the easiest bridge to make, and the one which is most economical, is some form of trestle bridge.

Where the bottom cannot be touched, for small spans the single lock, double lock or cantilever bridge may be used, or, if

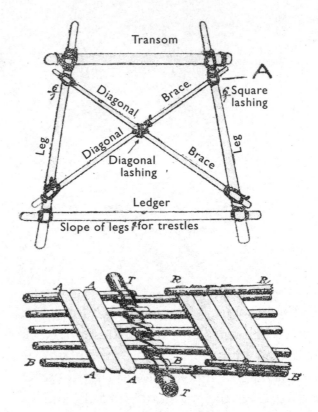

floating material is handy and the water and current suitable, a floating bridge is simple and quick to make.

There is no use discussing here bridges suitable for long spans where the bottom cannot be touched, as such bridges require skilled labour and huge quantities of material.

Bridges, of course, may be a combination of any of the above. For instance, we might form trestles across a stream till the water gets too deep, and use floating piers for the centre of the bridge.

Scouts should practise making model trestle bridges. For the spars, excellent material can be had from the nearest poulterer. The hickory skewers used to trussing fowls will be found admirable for the purpose. The bottoms of match-boxes can be used for the roadway as chesses.

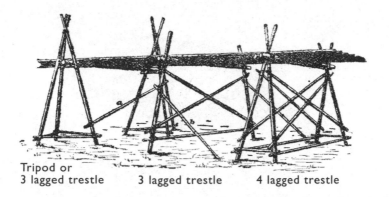

Tripod or
3 lagged trestle   3 lagged trestle   4 lagged trestle

SINGLE LOCK BRIDGE

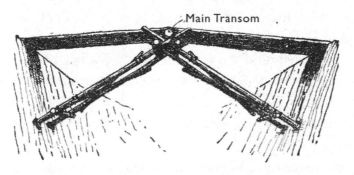

Main Transom

DOUBLE LOCK BRIDGE

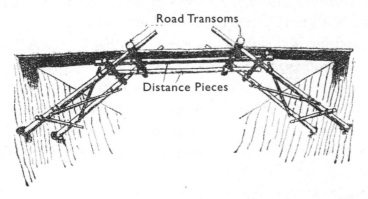

Road Transoms

Distance Pieces

VARIOUS STYLES OF BRIDGES MADE WITH TRESTLES
OR OTHERWISE

Hut Building: Temporary huts may be made from brushwood, straw, reeds, rushes, turf and stones.

Any available pieces of timber should be kept for doors and floors of the hut, unless sufficient is available for the whole hut.

The floors should be covered with planks of wood if available; or if wood is not available, with an inch or two of dry gravel or burned clay.

The minimum space for one person to sleep in a hut is two feet by six.

The drainage round the hut must be very carefully attended to, otherwise the inside will always be damp and musty, and in very wet weather the sides may fall in. A trench should be dug round the hut, sloped in such a way that no water will remain standing in it.

If the hut is to be slept in, a passage way should be sunk in the centre; this prevents people walking over the side benches, which are thus kept clean for sleeping in. the passage should be covered with two or three inches of gravel or ashes to keep it dry.

A rough hut may be made with hurdles; the hurdles are as follows:

A line six feet long is measured on the ground and divided into nine equal parts. Ten pickets, each three feet six inches long, and about one inch in diameter, are required. The two stouter pickets are driven, one at each end of the line, and the remainder at the divisions. The web is now commenced, and by the process of randing is continued to the height of one foot three inches, when pairing rods are introduced. The randing is then continued to the height of two feet six inches, when two more pairing rods are put on and the hurdle sewn in three places. Care should be taken that the stitches of the sewings enclose the centre pairing rods. The hurdle is now withdrawn from the ground, and after being reversed and refixed, two more pairing rods are put on and sewn as before. The ends of the pickets should be now cut to a uniform length of three feet and pointed, and all small twigs should be removed.

To make the Hut: The hurdles may be arranged on end in two rows nine feet apart, and the tops allowed to drop inwards to form a roof with a pitch of three feet six inches. The ends on the ground surface will require to be secured at frequent intervals by means of pickets. A light facine or pole should extend along the ridge in order to facilitate thatching, or other means of carrying off rainfall. Two shallow trenches should be cut along the eaves to form an eaves' gutter and at the same time drain the floor space.

Double-hurdle walls with earth or clay between them are much stronger, but they require a great deal of material.

After the hurdles are in position, they should be covered with clay or earth and brushwood.

Camp Kitchen: Dig a trench 6 to 8 feet long. It should be 6 inches deep under the position where the chimney is to be and slope down to 18 inches deep at the other end. The trench should be 6 inches wide at first; this will be increased by a couple of inches or so when the trench is trimmed. The ends of the trenches should be widened and in wet weather a drain made there.

To make the drain, dig a hole about 6 inches deep and fill in with stones.

The chimney should be about 4 or 5 feet high, the opening at the top being about 6 to 8 inches across. It should be made of sods or stones and all openings in the sides covered with clay or earth, well rammed in. when the wall of the chimney crosses the trench, it should be supported on large stones, bricks or slate.

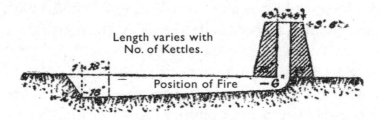

Length varies with No. of Kettles.

Position of Fire

PIPER BADGE

A Scout must be able to play a march and a reel on the pipes and dance the sword-dance.

There are numerous excellent "self-tutors" published for pipers, but it is almost impossible to learn the pipe properly without the assistance of a good teacher.

As a rule, anyone who tries to learn to play without a teacher develops a number of faults that are very difficult to get rid of later on.

As piping is learned and played practically entirely by ear, it is almost useless for anyone who has not a correct ear for music attempting to learn.

The beginner first learns to play on the practice chanter. This instrument costs from 5/- to 7/6.

It has eight holes, one at the top behind and seven in front, which allows of a scale of nine notes.

The chanter is held in both hands, left uppermost, with the holes straight to the front.

The thumb of the left hand covers the hole at the back; three fingers of the left hand cover the top three holes, and the four fingers of the right hand cover the four lower holes. The little finger on the left hand is not used at all, and the thumb of the right hand is only used to hold the instrument.

In the case of the left hand, the tip of the finger should be flat on the holes. With the right hand, however, the fingers are placed further across until the second joints of the fingers cover the holes. The fingers should be flat over the holes, and not curved round the chanter.

The fingers must completely cover the holes. This is not so easy as it sounds, and a beginner's first difficulty is to keep the holes covered.

After the scale is learned, short tunes may be tried.

When the beginner has fully mastered the scale and can play one or two short easy tunes, they may start to learn to play the grace notes or doubling. It is impossible to describe on paper how to double. This can only be learned from an instructor.

When the beginner has fully mastered the chanter, he may begin to blow the pipes.

A set of pipes costs from £3 10s. to £6.

They consist of three drones (a large one and two smaller ones), the blowpipe, the chanter and the bag.

Pipes should never be allowed to lie in the sun or in a draught, because if the bag gets dry, the reeds become harsh, and the bag leaks when the leather is dry.

The pipes should be kept in a cool place, slightly damp if possible; and to prevent the bag getting dry, they should be blown for a quarter of an hour every day.

PLUMBER BADGE

A Scout must be able to make wiped and brazed joints, to cut and fix a window pane, repair a burst pipe, mend a ball or faucet tap, and understand the ordinary hot-and-cold water system of a house and know how to protect exposed pipes against frost.

This is not an easy badge to get, and the best advice I can give to a Scout who wishes to get the badge is to make friends with the nearest plumber and get some practical information from him.

Understand the Hot-and-Cold Water system of a house: The hot-and-cold water system of a house will be best understood by reference to the drawings given below. These show the hot and cold pipes on a house of three stories. You have the main supply on the outside with a branch off to supply the house; this pipe rises straight to the attic to the storage cistern. Branches are taken from this pipe to the various fittings. From the storage cistern a pipe is taken to the boiler for the supply of hot water to the house. The boiler and hot-water storage tank or cylinders are connected by means of two pipes, called revolvers. The top one is called the flow, and the hot water in the boiler travels up this pipe to the cylinder; the cold water travels from cylinder by the lower or return pipe. From the top of the cylinder a pipe is taken off; this goes to the top of the house, and is taken through the attic and out onto the roof at a level some feet above the storage cistern. This pipe is called the expansion, and acts as a safety valve; if no outlet was provided, the water on being heated would expand to such an extent that it would burst the cylinder or some of the pipes.

COLD WATER SYSTEM

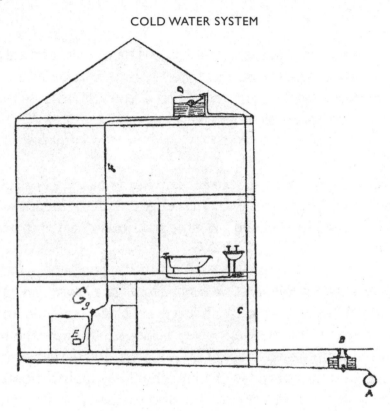

A Company's main pipe.
B Stopcock controlling house supply.
C Rising main in house.
D Cistern for storage.
E Boiler of kitchen range.
F Feed pipe to boiler.
G Stopcock controlling supply to boiler.

HOT WATER SYSTEM

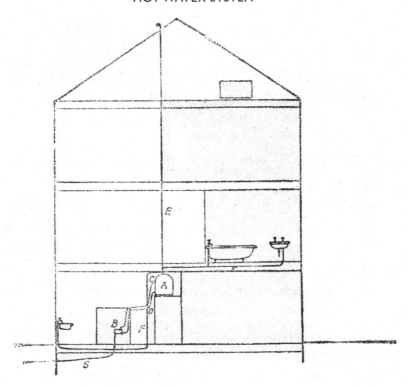

A Cylinder or hot-water storage tank.
B Boiler of kitchen range.
C Flow revolver.
D Return revolver.
E Expansion pipe.
F Branches to fittings.

POULTRY FARMER BADGE

A Scout must have a knowledge, gained by practice, of incubators, foster mothers, sanitary fowl-houses, and coops and runs; also of rearing, feeding, killing and dressing birds for market; also, he must be able to pack birds and eggs for market.

The best months for starting poultry keeping are November and December.

The first thing to do is select and prepare the ground, and to build the hen-roosts. Hen-houses and runs should be on ground as dry as possible; in a sheltered position and facing the south, so that the birds get as much sun as possible. If the ground is not naturally dry, it should be well drained. Damp ground soon becomes an unhealthy puddle.

The hen-house must be free from draughts. Draughty houses and damp ground are the certain causes of illness among the birds. It should also be protected from rats and mice by running some wirenetting, with $1/2$-inch mesh, right round. This netting should be sunk about 18 inches into the ground.

The size of the house depends, of course, on the number of hens that are to be kept. Before building the house, the foundations should be levelled and covered with 5 or 6 inches of coarse ashes. The roof should slope from front to rear, and the back should overlap the back wall by 6 inches or so to allow the rain to run off. The floors should be made of cement or of a mixture of tar, slaked lime, and small stones and sand mixed together to a good working consistency. This should be put on about 6 inches deep.

The most important thing, however, to see to in a hen-house, is ventilation. If the hen-houses are too warm, the fowls get overheated at night, and are then very liable to catch cold on going out in the morning. The main point is to have a ventilator that can be regulated according to the weather, and one that will not cause a draught. A ventilator fixed at the to answers the purpose well, provided it can be opened and shut. The hole where the fowls go in and out acts as a bottom ventilator.

The laying nests should be placed in the darkest portion of the house; this will naturally be under the window. Some old boxes, such as orange boxes, may be used for laying nests. Divide them into compartments and fill these with hay, putting a nest-egg in each. The hay should be changed at least once a month, and the boxes sprinkled with disinfectant.

A small piece of camphor tied in a piece of cloth and hung up in the hen-house is an excellent thing.

Having got the hen-house and run in perfect order, the next thing to do is to buy the stock of fowls. There are numerous varieties, and the breed selected must depend on whether the object is to sell the eggs or to hatch out chickens for table use.

Undoubtedly, the best layers are Minorcas. These fowls lay about 200 eggs each, per annum; but there are many other good egg producers, such as Plymouth Rocks, Scotch Greys, Hamburghs, Leghorns etc. For table use, the white-fleshed fowls are the best, such as the Dorking and game fowls. For general use, however, a first cross from any of the laying and table breeds is preferable. The cross-bred fowl is stronger and thrives better than the pure-bred fowl.

Feeding: Care should be taken not to overfeed the birds. This is a far more common fault than underfeeding.

Before laying the food in troughs, the beginner should first learn how much food the fowls require. To find this out, throw some food on the ground in small quantities, and when the fowls seem rather lazy in running after the food, stop giving any more. Only throw down what the fowls will run after and pick up greedily. Two good meals a day are all that are necessary; prepared soft food in the morning and grain at night. When penned up, garden refuse etc. should be given them to work among during the day in order to keep them active. The morning food should contain nettles, dandelions, and watercress. Dandelions act on the liver, while nettles keep the fowls' blood cool in spring.

Prepare the food as follows: Take some sprays of each and boil them among the potatoes, mix up well together, and add meal till the mixture is of a crumbly consistency.

At midday, give them a turnip cut through the centre or a grassy clod to peck at. When birds are laying a large number of eggs, they require some extra nourishment. A little meat cut up small and given with the soft food in the morning is necessary to their health. Onions are a preventative of disease and also help the birds to lay. A fair-sized onion is sufficient between six birds. It should be given raw, sliced up into small pieces, and mixed with their morning meal three times a week. Twice weekly, a little bone meal should be given. Salt should also be added to the soft food in the morning.

Hatching: After the hen-houses have been built and the stock of fowls purchased, the coops and runs for hatching purposes should be gone on with. The roof of the coop should slope from front to rear, and project about an inch beyond the sides and back, so as to carry off the rain. Avoid damp ground, and select a sheltered position facing the sun.

Each hen should be placed in a separate coop with a run, which should be wired in. The run should also be covered with small-meshed wire netting to prevent sparrows entering the run and eating the food. The nest should be made of earth, firmly beaten down, and hollowed in the centre. The hollow should be just deep enough to allow the eggs to roll gently towards the centre, so that should the hen displace any of the eggs when she gets out of the nest to feed, they will roll back into it. Sufficient soft hay should be put into the nest to keep the eggs off the earth.

On the eighth day of the hen's sitting, the eggs should be examined to see if they are fertile or unfertile; that is to say, whether they will eventually hatch into chickens or not. To find this out, cut an oval hole in a piece of cardboard, rather smaller than the size of the egg, hold the cardboard in one hand in front of a strong light, then hold the egg between the thumb and finger of the other hand against the oval hole. If the egg is fertile a dark central spot will be see this is called the germ; from this, radiating in all directions, there can be seen small fibres like the threads of a spider's web – those are the blood vessels of the unformed chicken.

If the egg looks clear all through it is unfertile and should be taken away from the next. Unfertile eggs need not be thrown away altogether, however; if removed at once they make good food for young chickens.

The chicks should be hatched out on the twenty-second day. The hen should be gently and quietly lifted, and taken away for a little. See that no chickens cling to her feather. Then carefully collect all the chicks, remove the eggshells and nest, and then place the hen over the brood.

After a little while, put some food in the run. The first meal should be hard-boiled eggs chopped up and mixed with breadcrumbs or oatmeal. After laying the food out for them, it is best to go away and leave them to come out themselves for the food.

Fattening Birds for Market: The fowls intended for market should be kept in coops, placed in a quiet corner away from a draught. Small feeding troughs should be fastened on to the outside of the coops, within easy reach of the bird. The food given for the first week should be four parts oats, ground as fine as possible, husks and all, one part barley meal, one part maize meal and one part bean meal. The meals should be mixed together with sufficient hot water to bring it to a fair consistency. After the first week, the meal should be mixed with half milk and half water, and a teaspoonful of melted butter added for each bird. The fowls for fattening should be fed three times a day.

Killing Fowls: Fowls should have no food for at least twelve hour before killing, and it is even better not to let them have food for twenty-four hours. The birds do not keep so long if killed immediately after a big meal. To kill a fowl, take the legs in the left hand, draw out the wings and grasp them also in the left hand, catch the neck smartly with the right hand, thumb pressed firmly in at the back of the head; at the same time place the neck and upper part of the breast over the right knee then give a good firm pull. The vertebral column is thus broken, and the fowl is killed practically without pain.

Plucking: The fowl should be plucked immediately after killing, as it is much easier plucked then than if allowed to get cold. In plucking, draw the feather out towards the tail. After plucking, the small young feathers have to be removed. This process is called "stubbing".

After the birds are cleaned, they should be allowed to hang for an hour or two to let them get firm. The carcase should then be lightly singed all over with burning paper, taking care, however, not to blacken it with smoke.

Packing Eggs for Market: Wrap each egg in a piece of soft paper, and pack in the box with soft hay. Hay is much better for packing than chaff or sawdust, as it is more elastic. Special egg boxes can be had, with separate divisions for each egg. The eggs should be wrapped in paper as above before being placed in the divisions. Mark the box, "Eggs with care."

Packing Fowls for Market: Turn the head neatly back over the side, double the legs in at each side of the body, and pin them in position. Wrap the fowls up on clean sheets of white paper, and pack in good clean straw. The straw keeps the birds fresh and clean.

PRINTER BADGE

A Scout must know the names of different types and paper sizes; be able to compose by hand or machine; understand the use of hand or power printing machines.

He must also print a handbill set up by himself.

Names of Types: The following is a list of the types most used in printing: English, Pica, Small Pica, Long Primer, Bourgeois, Brevier, Minion, Nonpareil, and Ruby. This book is composed in Minion Type.

Sizes of Printing Papers

Post, $19^{1}/4$" by $15^{1}/2$"
Medium, 24" by 19"
Demy, $22^{1}/2$" by $17^{1}/2$"
Royal 25" by 20"
Super-Royal, $27^{1}/2$" by $20^{1}/2$"
Imperial, 30" by 22"
Double Foolscap, 27" by 17"
Double Crown, 30" by 20"
Double Post, $31^{1}/2$" by $19^{1}/2$"
Double Demy, 35" by $22^{1}/2$"

Before the Scout commences setting or composing types, he must have some slight knowledge of the different material used.

Types: A type is a piece of metal or wood, rectangular in shape, and having cast or cut in relief on one (the top) of its six sides the distinctive design it is to impress. Types for bookwork are invariably cast in metal, only large types such as are used in posters or placards being cut in wood. Types are very much in depth and width, but whether they be small ones or large ones they are all of a uniform height. This height is somewhat less than an inch.

The character that each type is intended to impress is called the "face" of the type.

In typography, each type bears on its face one, and generally only one, character; in other words, every letter, point and sign is a distinctive type, and words and sentences are formed by placing the appropriate types together side by side in a line.

Doubtless, the Scout who is to be examined in this test has handled types, and has noticed that each letter has a nick or notch cut in the body or shank. The use of this nick is twofold. It enables the compositor to know by feel which is the bottom of the letter, and it also distinguishes between types of the same size, which may have been cast by different typefounders.

COMPOSING STICK

The reader will have noticed that in every book there are white spaces between the words. These are provided for by placing after the type that prints the last letter of each word, one or more pieces of metal called spaces. Spaces are shaped just like types, save that they are not quite so high and have no "faces", therefore, if properly placed, they never give any impression. Their only object is to keep types apart that would otherwise lie together.

Spaces have always the same depth as the types with which they are used. They vary in width, and each width has its name – thick, middle and thin.

The wider spaces are called "quadrats" or "quads". They are generally used for the purpose of producing the white spaces which usually occur at the ends of sentences and paragraphs. Like the spaces, they are always of the same depth as they type with which they are used, but are of various widths.

TYPE CASES

PROSPECTOR BADGE

> A Scout must have a general knowledge of the various periods
> of the formation of the earth's crust and which are water-bearing
> rocks. Must understand stratification, dip and faults. Must be able to
> identify:
>   (a) Twenty different minerals in their natural state;
>   (b) Twenty different fossils, and know to what period they belong.

The subjects included in this badge principally refer to that part of geology called Pioneer Work; that is, being able to write a report on any part of a country, which has been roughly surveyed by simply walking over it and noting the nature of the surface rocks and where any strata come to the surface; being able to state where water is likely to be found; and tracing certain strata which dip under the surface to where they appear again, or being able to say where they are likely to crop out.

Taking a walk over a stretch of country, and examining the rocks and soil as we go along, we find them of many kinds, but one feature is that they are mostly lying in beds, or strata, as if laid down one on the top of the other.

The rocks of the earth's crust, as we can prove by examination, have mostly been laid down in this way, and the total thickness of strata is about 25 miles.

Volcanoes and earthquakes and vast upheavals of the earth-surface have lifted the oldest rocks over the youngest, and in this manner we can view the total thickness of rock laid down. The molten matter ejected by volcanoes, which has come up in vast quantities through fissures in the crust, are now to be seen as what is called igneous rocks, that is, those which have not been deposited by water, etc.

All this mass of strata is divided into periods, named by the traces of life found in it, or by the fossils which characterise it. the following table shows the oldest rocks at the bottom to the newest rocks at the top, and the name given to each period:

Post Tertiar
Recent
Prehistoric
Pleistocene

Tertiary or Cainozoic
Pliocene
Miocene
Oligocene
Eocene

Secondary or Mesozoic
Cretaceous
Jurassic
Triassic

Primary or Palæozoic
Permian
Carboniferous
Devonian
Silurian
Cambrian
Pre-Cambrian

Stratification: which we have mentioned, is one of the branches of constructive geology, and one of the most interesting. The name expresses the leafing structural features belonging to sedimentary rocks.

Faults: The movements which the crust of the earth has undergone have folded and fractured the rocks in all directions; and where the stratum has broken, one side having been displaced from the other, a fault is said to occur. There are many kinds of faults, which are named after the manner in which the rocks have been moved.

Fossils: These are traces of life in former ages, and are usually found in sedimentary rocks; that is, rocks formed by the deposition of matter in water. They usually consist of bones, shells, teeth of animals, bark, wood, leaves etc., also footprints or tracks, and moulds of the soft parts of animals. Fossils are classified in the animal and vegetable kingdoms, and are rarely the same as present forms of life, although being somewhat like them.

To study the many forms of life preserved to us, it is necessary to have a knowledge of living forms and their classification.

The study of ancient life is a very large subject, and cannot be done without having access to a collection; or a small collection can be purchased by the student. It would be impossible to give drawings of the many types of fossil-remains, and, indeed, that would prove but a poor way of learning this absorbing subject. We can only give a piece of advice, that is, to visit the nearest museum and get friendly with the caretaker or person in charge of the collection.

We give the principal epochs now, with the characteristic fossils found in each, as a very elementary guide to follow up in the collection:

Cambrian – Trilobites are the foremost group found here, of which there are three types, Olenellus, Paradoxides and Olenus.
Silurian – Corals are found as Favosites (i.e. honeycomb), Heliolites (i.e. the sun).
Devonian – A shell called Clymenia.
Carboniferous – So called from the fact that it contains our coal beds.

Stigmaria – These are trees and roots.

Permian – Land plants, as Lepidodendron.

Triassic – A fossil fish Ceratodus.

Jurassic – Shells, as Ammonites; Belemnites are abundant.

Cretaceous – Sea Urchins, Holaster and Micraster.

Eocene – Plants, as Pandanus; shells, as Voluta.

Oligocene – Shells, as Astarte. The horse also appears in this series.

Pleistocene – Here are human remains and bones with carving on them.

The story of these ancient forms of life is most interesting, and no better way can be found of studying them than by making frequent visits to a museum.

List of Minerals

Copper Pyrites	Iron Pyrites	Hematite
Tinstone	Blende	Galena
Quartz, crystallised	Quartz, massive	Mica
Felspar	Dolomite	Fluor Spar
Calc Spar, crystal	Calc Spar, massive	Rock Salt
Baryta, crystal	Baryta, massive	Gypsum
Selenite	Hornblende	Gneiss
Syenite	Granite	Shale
Limestone	Feltstone	Limestone (marble)
Eucrinitol (marble)	Coralline (marble)	

List of Fossils

Red Crag.	Fusus antiquus (var. contrarius)
	Pectunculus glycimoris
White Crag.	Cardita senitis
Eocene.	Voluta, sp., or Chama squamosal
	Nummulites, sp.
	Crassatella sulcata, or
Chalk.	Micraster, sp., or Galerites, sp.
	Ptychodus (tooth). Jurritella granulata
Greensand.	Terebratula Liplicata
Gault.	Inocerancus salcatus. Ammonites splendeus
Oolite.	Injonia impressa. Terebratula digona
Lias.	Ammonites communis
	Rhynconelia tetrahedral; or Gryphæa, sp
	Pentarineus briareus
Coal Measure	Fern or Shale
Mountain Limestone	Productus, sp.
Silurian	Spririfer, sp. (or) Atrypa reticularis
	Grapholite, sp.
	Phacops, sp.

PUBLIC HEALTH MAN BADGE

A Scout must:

Know the dangers of scarlet fever, diphtheria and tuberculosis; showing how they are transmitted and the best methods to prevent them spreading.

Give a list of all infectious diseases that must be notified, and the precautions that must be taken to prevent the infection spreading; state also the period of incubation of each disease.

Describe one or more methods of disinfecting a house and a room and its contents after a contagious disease.

Describe the necessity of and the mode employed in his own locality for the collection, removal and destruction of house refuse and rubbish.

Have a general knowledge of the laws (general and local) governing dairies, dairyfarms, slaughterhouses and butcher's shops.

Scarlet Fever: A highly infectious disease. Incubation period one to seven days, usually three. Six weeks is the usual period and the patient should be in quarantine for ten days after the skin has peeled. The disease may be followed by ulceration of the throat, discharge from the ears, inflamed neck glands and inflammation of the kidneys.

Infection is spread by contact and proximity to a patient. The germ is retained in infected clothing etc. for months. Infection is carried in milk. The health authorities must be at once advised, and often they may be able to trace the source to a dairy, and thereby stop the epidemic.

Diphtheria: Is a disease due to bad sanitation. This disease never attacks a person in good health, but one whose system has been lowered by a vitiated atmosphere, and by the escape of sewage gas into the room. Incubation period, one to seven days, usually two; quarantine, eight days after the total disappearance of the spores.

Tuberculosis: Attacks the lungs, glands and bones. Consumption is the result of this bacillus attacking the lungs and is the cause of more suffering and death than any other disease. A consumptive patient expectorates a great deal of phlegm containing thousands of germs. Obviously, the spread of consumption can be prevented by the proper disposal of this expectoration. It should not be allowed to remain on floors, or anywhere where it might become dry. It should be washed into the sewers or burned. Each patient should have small rags into which he can expectorate, and they should be thrown into the fire as soon as possible. Small pocket spittoons can be purchased, which are emptied frequently.

As many people suffer from consumption without knowing it, the regulation in most large towns, "Don't Spit", should be rigorously enforced.

Membraneous Croup: Is similar to diphtheria, which see above.

Smallpox: Incubation period, twelve days; quarantine, eight days after disappearance of all skin particles. This loathsome disease is now happily rare in this country, and the slight epidemics which occasionally break out are usually easily supressed by the local medical authorities.

Typhus: An infectious epidemic disease, attacks squalid neighbourhoods, which are filthy and overcrowded and ill-ventilated, and where the inhabitants are poorly fed. Preventative measures are therefore obvious. To those living in well-ventilated, airy houses it is practically innocuous.

Typhoid (or Enteric Fever): Infection is caused through coming in contact with the excretions from a patient suffering from the disease. The excretions may contaminate a water supply and cause an epidemic. If they are carefully disposed of and not allowed to contaminate food, clothing or bedclothes, there is little risk of infection. Cases can usually be traced to infection from milk, shellfish (such as oysters), watercress, ice cream, etc. which have somehow got contaminated with sewage water. Flies also are responsible for carrying the microbes of this and other diseases.

Puerperal Fever: Is a form of blood-poisoning which occurs in women in childbirth through neglect and want of cleanliness or the use of unclean instruments.

Relapsing Fever (or Famine Fever): A contagious form of continued fever. It was one time very prevalent in Ireland. It is found especially in connection with famines where the inhabitants have undergone privations and great shortage of food.

Cholera: Is, fortunately, very rare in this country. Infection is got from excretions from a patient coming into contact with water supply, food etc. Rats are a means of spreading the disease.

Erysipelas: Is a contagious disease and is transferable from person to person. No delicate person, especially with any broken skin, should remain near the patient.

Spread of infection: Cleanliness of person, home, furniture and surroundings; abundant fresh air and free and abundant ventilation are the best preventatives. Closed windows are a sure forerunner of disease. Exclusion of all foetid gases from dwelling-house. A pure water and milk supply. Most of the infectious diseases are spread by infected water and milk.

Flies are largely responsible for spreading infectious diseases. They thrive and breed in manure heaps, stable refuse etc. Removal of this refuse and the campaign of "Kill That Fly" has greatly helped in lessening the spread of infectious diseases. Still a great deal more can be done in destroying flies and their breeding grounds.

SEA FISHERMAN BADGE

A Scout must have a practical knowledge of the various methods of catching fish for the market by means of trawls, nets and lines, and of catching shellfish. He must have had experience of at least three of these methods, one of which shall be by the trawl, and must know the Mercantile Code of signals.

VARIOUS METHODS OF CATCHING FISH

SIGNALLER BADGE

A Scout:

1. Must pass tests in both sending and receiving in Semaphore and Morse signalling by flag. Minimum rate of 24 letters per minute for Morse, 36 for Semaphore.

2. Give and read signals by sound. Make correct smoke and flame signals with fires.

3. Show off the proper method of signalling with the staff as in *Scouting for Boys*.

Semaphore

At the start, every Scout should realise that after a little practise anyone can easily read the Semaphore, provided it is accurately sent; that is to say, provided that the signaller attends strictly to the following points:

(i) He must stand exactly facing the person or station he is sending to, firmly on both feet, the feet to be 8 to 10 inches apart.

(ii) The flags must be held at the full extent of the arms, and the arm and flag must form one straight line. A good plan is to push the end of the pole up under the sleeves, and have the first finger of each hand lying along the pole.

(iii) Don't throw the arms to the rear.

(iv) Be very careful to place the arms in the exact positions for the letters. This is the most important point. Bad or careless sending is impossible to read, and the commonest error is not paying strict attention to this point.

(v) Letters A, B, and C, must only be made with the right hand and letters E, F, G, must only be made with the left hand. Never bring the arms across the body to form these letters.

(vi) Both flags must be of the same colour, and the sender must see that he is standing behind a background of uniform colour. The question of backgrounds will be referred to later on.

(vii) In sending letters where the flags are close together, such as O and W, the flags must be kept separate and not allowed to cover one another.

(viii) When forming letters when both flags are the same side of the body, such as the letters O, X, W etc., the signaller should turn well around on the hips, but keeping his head and eyes straight to the front. The flags should also be on the same plane, that is to say, one should be exactly above the other.

(ix) When double letters occur, the flags should be brought well into the body. Don't attempt the peculiar juggling performance that is sometimes done for double letters. In fact, never use out-of-the-way means of trying to send faster, as they only lead to confusion.

(x) Don't' send too fast, and never send faster than it is within the powers of the reader to read without confusion. Doing this only means waste of time, through repetitions etc.

(xi) When at the "ready position", or when or when making letters that require the use of only one arm, the flags should be kept right in front of the body, the point of the poles pressing against the legs.

How to Learn Semaphore: The Scout should first be shown the correct angles at which to hold the flags, as shown in the picture opposite. The easiest method to learn the alphabet is by circles.

1st Circle	A to G.
	A, B, and C sent with the right hand only.
	D with either hand.
	E, F, and G, with the left hand.
2nd Circle	H to N omitting J.
	Learners sometimes experience a little difficulty with this circle by forgetting that J is missed out. In this circle the right hand is held at the position for the letter A, the left hand only being moved in this circle.
3rd Circle	O to S.
	The right hand at position for letter B, the left hand only being moved.
4th Circle	T, U, Y, and Erase.
	The right hand at position for letter C, the left hand only being moved.
5th Circle	Numeral sign J (or alphabetical sign), and V.
	The right hand at position for letter D, the left hand only being moved.
6th Circle	W and X.
	The left hand at position for letter E, the right hand in this case moving down 45 degrees to show letter X.

7th Circle   Z.
              When the Scout is able to go through the alphabet
              correctly, he should practise sending a letter and its
              opposite;

For instance, H is opposite to Z,
               P is opposite to J,
               O is opposite to W, and so on.

It cannot be too often repeated that sending is far more important than reading. Reading can easily be learned with a little practise, but a bad style of sending is easily acquired; and once acquired it is difficult to get into the correct style.

Never send in a slovenly manner. Move the flags smartly from one position to another. Carefully study the diagrams and get into the habit of moving the arms into the exact positions.

The best way of learning to read is to get a good signaller to send to you. If you can't get a good signaller, the next best way is to get a packet of Semaphore Signalling Cards as published by Messrs James Brown & Son. These cards are very useful for practising at odd moments when it is not possible to get someone to send.

Don't practise reading by signalling before a mirror. The letters are reversed and will only confuse you when you try to read an actual signaller. The only point of using a mirror is to see if you are placing the arms in the exact positions.

How to send a message in Semaphore: In sending words or groups of letters, the arms are brought down to the "ready" position after each word or group.

The arms are not brought down to the ready position after

each letter, but moved smartly to the position for each letter in the word, making a pause in each letter according to the rate of sending. If the arm is already in position to form, or assist to form, the next letter in the word, it will be kept steady. For instance, take the word "milkman". The right arm is at position for letter A all through the word, and does not require to be moved; the left hand only in this case forming the different letters.

To Call Up: Place the hands in the position for the letter J and move the flags, using the wrists only. This is answered by the receiving station sending the letter J without moving the flags.

When sending a message, the sender should have someone to read the message to him, and the reader someone to write it for him. The reader should read each letter and never attempt to try to guess the word. This only leads to mistakes.

The reader should call out each letter in a loud voice, and when the sender comes down to the ready position, the reader says "group", which informs the writer that it is the end of a word or group.

Everyone will find that some of the letters in the alphabet are very a like in sound when called out; for instance, it is often very difficult to distinguish between M and N or B and C, etc. For this reason, some of the letters are given names. They are as follows:

A is called ac.	S is called esses.
B is called beer.	T is called toc.
M is called emma.	V is called vic. P is called pip.

Signallers must get into the habit of using these names when reading out a message.

At the end of each word or group, the sender comes down to the "ready". If the reader has read correctly, he sends a single dash (that is like the letter T in Morse). If the reader has not read the message, he makes no sign and the sender repeats the word or group.

At the end of every message, the sender will send V E (in one group) meaning "very end". If the receiving station is satisfied that they have received the message correctly, they will send R D (in one group), the first and last letters in the word "received", meaning message received.

Morse

In the Morse system, letters are formed by what are termed "dots" and "dashes".

In signalling, these signs are conveyed by several different means, but the difference is quite easily distinguished by the time taken in making them. Whatever the means used, or whatever the rate of sending, the dash is always three times the length of a dot. This is a most important point, and must be strictly attended to.

By this system, the letters may be represented by the short and long waves of a flag, the short or long exposures of the light of a lamp, by short or long blows of whistles etc., or by sound as with a "tapper", "buzzer", or telegraph sounder.

Whatever means of transmission is used, the following points must be strictly adhered to:

1. A dash is three times the length of a dot.

2. A pause of time equal to the time of a dash must be made at the end of each letter.

3. A letter must be made continuously from start to finnish, without any interval between the elements composing it. This must be done so as to prevent a letter being misread as two or more other letters. For instance, the letter C is -- • -- •, and the letter N is -- •; therefore, if a pause was made after the first dot in C it would be read as two "N's".

4. Always, no matter what the rate of sending is, make an appreciable pause at the bottom of the dash. Never pause at the top until the end of the letter.

5. Bring the flag back smartly to the "Prepare to Signal" after each word or group, holding the flag into the body with the left hand.

6. The signaller must stand exactly facing, or with his back to, the distant station, according to the direction of the wind; but, whatever the latter, he must stand square, so that he can wave the flag at right angles to the line of sight to the distant station.

7. The pole must be kept upright and the point not allowed to droop to the front or rear, so that the flag is waved in a vertical plane, and not swept round to front, or overhead.

8. The pole must be held at the extremity of the butt.

9. All motions of the flag must be sharp; both whilst signalling and in moving from one position to another.

10. The flag must be kept fully exposed when sending; it must at other times be completely hidden from the view of the distant station.

11. The dots and dashes must be uniform in length; and bear the correct proportion to one another.

Flag Drill: Prepare to signal. Carry the left foot about 10 inches to the left, cant the pole with the right hand upwards to the left, catching it with the left hand about the centre. At the same time, seize the pole with the right hand about six inches from the butt, then grasp the flag with the left hand in line with the right, both hands to be close together and level with the waist, the pole to point upwards across the left shoulder.

Dummy Key (see below): The sound made by it is similar to that of a telegraph sounder.

From the first, Scouts should be instructed in the reading from and sending on this instrument.

This is the best way to learn Morse. If a Scout can send and read the dummy key easily, he will find no difficulty in sending and reading by lamp, heliograph or buzzer.

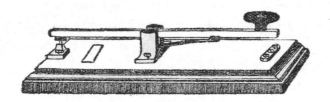

How to Learn Morse Alphabet: The Morse alphabet is so made up that those letters which occur most often in an English sentence are represented by the shortest symbols. Don't attempt to learn the alphabet until a correct method of sending dots and dashes has been acquired. An excellent method of practising is to send a series of dots and dashes continually until tired, never pausing at the top of the dot or dash, but always making an appreciable pause at the bottom of a dash.

The simplest way to learn the alphabet is as follows:

• E	— T (called toc)
• • I	— — M (called emma)
• • • • S (called esses)	— — — O
• • • • • H	

Opposites

A • — (called ac)			— •	N
B — • • • (called beer)			• • • —	V (called vic)
D — • •			• • —	U
F • • — •			• — • •	L
G — — •			• — —	W
Q — — • —			— • — —	Y

Sandwiches

K — • —	R • — •
P • — — • (called pip)	X — • • —

Letters with no Opposites

C — • — •   J • — — —   Z — — • •

Numerals

1 • —	4 • • • • —	7 — — • • •	
2 • • —	5 •	8 — • •	
3 • • • — —	6 — • • • •	9 — •	0 —

Figures are always preceded with FI (meaning figures intended) + followed by FF (meaning figures finished).

A good way to learn the alphabet, although on paper it looks very ridiculous, is to call dots "iddy", and dashes "umpty". This gives really the sound made by the tapper. For instance, take C, -- - -- -, it would be called "umpty iddy, umpty iddy", with a strong emphasis on the "umpty".

Learn E, I, S, H, and T, M, O first; they present no difficulty. Then try sending and reading words formed by those seven letters, such as: it, is, she, his, set, tom, met, hot, test, shoes, host, etc., until the letters are easily read and sent. Then, take the next two letters in the list, A and N, and make words with those, in conjunction with the seven letters already learned; then take two more letters; and so on. Don't try to learn too many letters at first, or you will only muddle yourself. Learn a few letters thoroughly, and don't proceed to the next letters until those ones are thoroughly mastered. In sending words, combine the letters last learned with the letters already known.

STALKER BADGE

A Scout must take a series of twenty photographs of wild animals or birds from life, and develop and print them himself, and must also be able to give particulars of their lives, habits and markings.

TRACKING WILD ANIMALS

STARMAN BADGE

A Scout must:

Have a general knowledge of the nature and movements of the stars.

Be able to point out and name six principal constellations.

Find the north by means of other stars than the Pole Star, in case of that star being obscured by clouds etc., and tell the hour of the night by the stars or moon.

Have a general knowledge of the positions and movements of the earth, sun and moon, and of tides, eclipses, meteors, comets, sun-spots, planets.

Were any boy to ask the writer which test he thought would afford the student greatest pleasure, he would at once answer, "The test for the Starman's Badge of Merit."

Our universe (as we call all the created things) is so wonderful, so awe-inspiring, that it almost seems too sacred to write about. Certainly, words can only convey a most infinitely small idea of the grandeur and majesty of the heavens. In this article description has been studiously avoided, and the writer has endeavoured to place before his readers a simple explanation of the wonders of the skies.

Let us study together. We shall begin with our own world. How was this world formed? Well, as there was nobody there at the time, we are apt to say that nobody knows. But not so fast! We have read of detectives finding little scraps of evidence and by piecing them together arriving at a conclusion. And that is what has happened with the history of our earth. Great thinkers, whom we call astronomers, have gathered evidence which they have pieced together. They have even watched and are still watching other worlds in the course of construction, just as ours was formed millions and millions of years ago. One of their different theories is something like this. All the matter which composes the sun and the other worlds was at one time one gigantic, shapeless mass of cloud (a nebula) floating through space and whirling at a tremendous rate. Gradually, bits separated from this enormous cloud and went journeying off "on their own", as we might say. These detached parts continued to whirl and, in course of time, became planets and satellites, revolving in different orbits round the sun.

Now, we ask, if in the beginning the earth did really break off this huge mass, why did it not fly away through space and get completely lost? To answer this, we must ask ourselves another question: when we throw a ball into the air why does it not fly away through space? It doesn't; it comes back to us. Something has drawn it back to the earth. That something is called the force of gravitation, a strange, mysterious force which makes every one thing in the universe attract every other. That is why we have not flown away from the sun; that is why the moon has not flown away from the earth; that is why the whole of our system remains compact.

But we must get on. You have all been taught at school what causes night and day; how the earth by revolving is continually presenting one side and then the other to the light of the sun, while the opposite side is in the shade. Now, as the earth spins, it also travels round the sun. It does not travel in a circle but is an ellipse (see opposite). During this travel round the sun the earth makes 365 turns, making, therefore, 365 days, which, as we know, makes a year. Did we hear someone say something about a leap year, which has 366 days? Well, thanks for the correction. It should really be 365 and one quarter turns it makes. But it would be an awful nuisance to have a quarter day occurring every year, so we disregard the quarter for four years and we find there is an extra day, so we tack it onto the shortest month, which is February, and give it twenty-nine days, which is a simple way out of the difficulty.

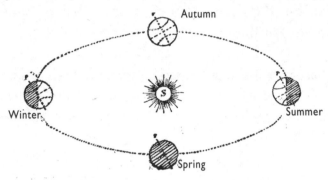

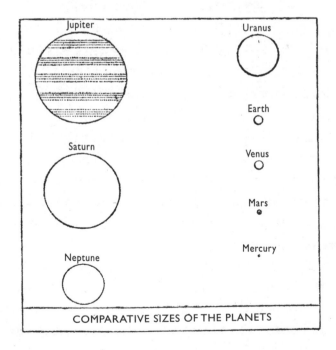

COMPARATIVE SIZES OF THE PLANETS

Now, it seems strange that as our earth travels, its servant the moon travels with it, but we saw how the taskmaster gravity keeps it near its mistress. The moon, however, not only moves with the earth in its journey round the sun, but revolves round the earth once a month as well.

The following is a list of the planets with their distances from the sun, the length of their years and the number of their moons. For their comparative sizes, see above.

Name of Planet	Miles from the Sun	Length of Year	Moons
Mercury	36,000,000	88 days	0
Venus	67,000,000	224 days	0
Earth	93,000,000	365 days	1
Mars	141,000,000	687 days	2
Jupiter	483,000,000	11 years 8	
Saturn	886,000,000	29 years 10	
Uranus	1,781,000,000	84 years	4
Neptune	2,791,000,000	164 years	1

By length of year, of course, we mean the length of time the planet takes to travel once around the sun.

But these eight planets do not make up the whole family of worlds of which the sun is the parent. There are a number of smaller planets, far smaller than the moon, which go round between Mars and Jupiter. They are very small, and all the hundreds of them put together would not make up one world the size of our own.

Again, the solar system includes a number of strange and wonderful objects which are utterly different from any of those we have been reading about. They are called comets. They also travel round the sun and, therefore, belong to the family.

Comets do not go round the sun in circles, but always in paths like a circle that has been rather flattened in one direction, like the path of the earth. In the case of comets, the ellipse (as this shape is called) is very extreme,.

It almost runs into the sun, but instead turns round it, then away on another journey of millions and millions of miles, far beyond even Neptune, and then the taskmaster gravity tells it that it should pay another visit home to its parent. Then the wanderer returns. It seems like a prodigal son, but still it is one of the family.

But what is this muddle we have got into? At one time, we are told that the sun, the centre of gravity, exerts a pulling influence on everything in the universe, and, the next minute, we are informed that the sun throws back the filmy substance from the comet's nucleus. But wait, there is no muddle at all. There is a force known as "radiation pressure"; that is, light has the power of pressing or pushing. It is possible to prove this by a very delicate experiment if you take a balance, for a flash of light will push down the end of the balance. It is this light pressure, or radiation pressure, that makes the tails of comets, and explains why the tail appears when the comet gets near the sun, and why it is always on the side away from the sun.

We already know that the sun is a star and the stars are suns. We also know that there are numberless fixed stars, among which the planets wander. Let us deal with these fixed stars. Long ago, men noticed that these stars did not change their positions, and they naturally came to group them together, and we call these groups constellations.

If we consider how the earth turns in space, we shall see that only half of the sky can be seen from our northern half of the earth. As it happens, this includes the most interesting and wonderful of the stars. Of these constellations, the best known,

I think, is the Plough, and it is useful for finding the north, we shall give it a special place here.

Here we see how to fix on the Pole star at once, and, as the Pole star is situated exactly over the terrestrial north pole, or nearly so, we have our northerly direction at once.

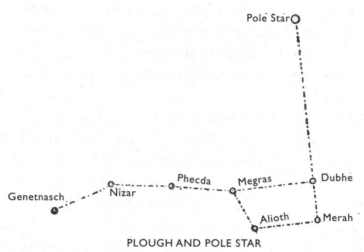

PLOUGH AND POLE STAR

In alphabetical order the constellations visible from our northern hemisphere are as follows:

NAME	MEANING
Andromeda	The Chained Lady
Aquila	The Eagle
Auriga	The Charioteer
Boötes	The Herdsman
Cassiopeia	The Lady in the Chair
Cepheus	King Cepheus
Cygnus	The Swan
Corona Borealis	The Northern Crown
Draco	The Dragon
Equuleus	The Little Horse

Hercules	The Kneeling Man
Lyra	The Harp
Ophiuchus	The Serpent Bearer
Pegasus	The Flying Horse
Sagitta	The Arrow
Serpens	The Serpent
Triangulum	The Triangle
Ursa Major	The Great Bear
Ursa MinorT	he Little Bear

These are the northern constellations as classified by Ptolemy at least 2,000 years ago. He also arranged the following southern constellations:

NAME	MEANING
Argo	The Ship Argo
Ara	The Altar
Corona Australis	The Southern Crown
Centaurus	The Centaur
Corvus	The Crow
Crater	The Cup
Cetus	The Whale
Canis Major	The Great Dog
Canis Minor	The Little Dog
Eridanus	The River
Hydra	The Snake
Lepus	The Wolf
Orion	The Hunter
Pisces	The Fishes

We shall now go stargazing. Just look at these five stars like a big W; what is that? That constellation is called:

The Stars of Spring

These Charts should be read from the outer circle (the horizon) to the centre, which represents the zenith (exactly overhead).

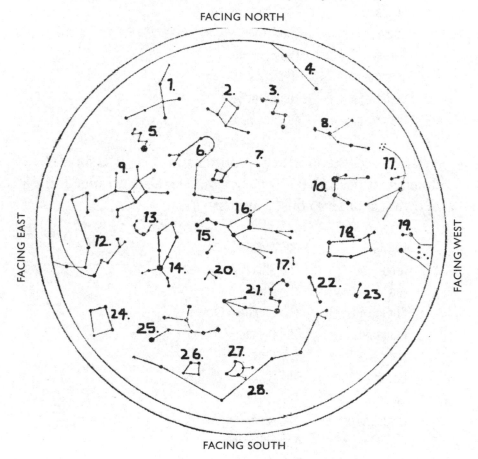

FACING NORTH

FACING EAST

FACING WEST

FACING SOUTH

1	Cygnus	15	Canes Venatici
2	Cepheus	16	Ursa Major
3	Cassiopeia	17	Lyra
4	Andromeda	18	Gemini with Pollax and Castor stars
5	Lyra with Vega star	19	Orion
6	Draco	20	Coma Bereniges
7	Ursa Minor with star Pole Star	21	Leo
8	Perseus with Algol star	22	Cancer
9	Hercules	23	Canis Minor with Procyon star
10	Auriga with Capella star	24	Libra
11	Taurus with Aldebarana star	25	Virgo with Spica star
12	Serpens with Ophiuchus star	26	Coryus
13	Corona	27	Crater
14	Bootes with Arcturus star	28	Hydra with Alphard star

The Stars of Summer

The stars rise about 4 minutes earlier every day, which makes a difference in their positions of about 2 hours each month.

FACING NORTH

FACING EAST

FACING WEST

FACING SOUTH

1	Auriga	16	Cygnus
2	Lynx	17	Lyra with Vega star
3	Perseus with Algol star	18	Hercules
4	Trianculum	19	Cornona
5	Andromeda	20	Bootes with Arcturus star
6	Cassiopeia	21	Virgo with Spica star
7	Ursa Major	22	Delphinus
8	Leo with Regulus star	23	Aquarius
9	Pisces	24	Aquilla with Altair star
10	Pegasus	25	Ophiuchus
11	Cepheus	26	Seapens
12	Ursa Minor with Pole Star	27	Libra
13	Draco	28	Capricornus
14	Canes Venatici	29	Sagittarius
15	Coma Berenicles	30	Scorpius with Antares star

The Stars of Autumn

For the positions of the "wandering" planets, see *Star Sheet Almanac* for the current year.

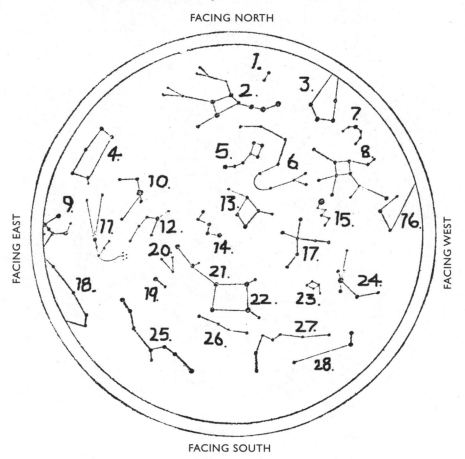

FACING NORTH

FACING EAST

FACING WEST

FACING SOUTH

1	Canes Venatici	15	Lyra with Vega star
2	Ursa Major	16	Ophiuchus
3	Bootes	17	Cygnus
4	Gemini with Polax and Castor stars	18	Eridanus
5	Ursa Minor with Pole Star	19	Aries
6	Draco	20	Triangulum
7	Corona	21	Andromeda
8	Hercules	22	Pegasus
9	Orion	23	Delphminus
10	Auriga with Capella star	24	Aquilla with Altair star
11	Taurus with Aldebaron and Pleiades stars	25	Cetus with Mira star
12	Pegasus with Algol star	26	Pisces
13	Cepheus	27	Aquarius
14	Cassiopeia	28	Capricornus

The Stars of Winter

FACING NORTH

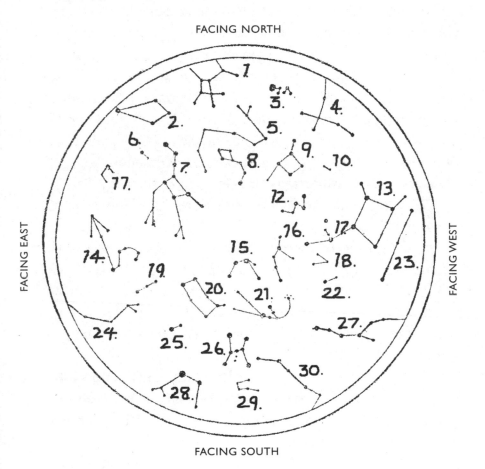

FACING EAST

FACING WEST

FACING SOUTH

1	Hercules	16	Peseus
2	Bootes with Arcturus star	17	Andromeda
3	Lyra with Vega star	18	Triangulum
4	Cygnus	19	Cancer
5	Draco	20	Gemini with Pollax and Castor stars
6	Canes Venatici	21	Taurus with Aldebaron and Pleiades stars
7	Ursa Major	22	Aries
8	Ursa Minor	23	Pisces
9	Cepheus	24	Hydra
10	Lagerta?	25	Canis Minor with Procyon star
11	Coma Berenicles	26	Orion
12	Cassiopeia	27	Cetus with Mira star
13	Pegasus	28	Canis Minor with Sirius star
14	Leo with Regulus star	29	Lepus
15	Auriga with Capetta star	30	Eridanus

Marching by the Stars

Sir Norman Lockyer, on referring to the soldier's need of being able to find his bearings in difficult night marches, reminds us that when Lord Wolseley ordered the night attack upon Arabi's forces at Tel-el-Kebir, the general in command was compelled to obtain the services of two naval officers who knew how to guide his army by the stars. "A similar situation," Sir Norman says, "might arise at any time," and adds that, "any moderately intelligent man can be taught enough about the stars to find his bearings and steer a course by the stars."

Aviators, sailors and Scouts are well aware of the value of the stars at night as guides.

In the daytime, the four points of the compass may always be known by ascertaining the sun's position at certain times of the day. About 6 a.m., it is due east; about 9, south east; at noon, south; at 3 p.m., south west; at 6 p.m., due west; but in the winter it will not have reached the western point before setting.

At night, when the stars are shining, the north and south points can be found from the North Polar Star, which is always due north, the east being on the right hand of the observer when facing the north, and the west on the left.

The direction may also be found from the full moon, which is opposite the sun. The shadow from a stick set up in the moonlight will tell the position of the sun, which at full moon is due west at 6 p.m., due north at midnight, and due east at 6 a.m.; and since the sun moves, apparently, 15 degrees every hour, its intermediate positions can be easily calculated. The sun's position being known, the time can also be roughly calculated.

SURVEYOR BADGE

A Scout must:

Map correctly, from the country itself, the main features of half a mile of road, with 440 yards each side, to a scale of two feet to the mile, and afterwards re-draw same map from memory.

Measure the heights of a tree, telegraph pole and church steeple, describing method adopted.

Measure width of a river, and distance apart of two objects a known distance away and unapproachable.

Be able to measure a gradient.

Understand what is meant by H.E., V.I., R.F., contours, conventional signs of Ordnance Survey and scales.

SWIMMER BADGE

A Scout must swim 50 yards with clothes on (shirts, trousers and socks as a minimum), and be able to undress in the water. He must swim (without clothes) 100 yards on the breast and 50 yards on the back with the hands either clasped or the arms folded in front of the body. He must be able to dive and pick up small objects from the bottom.

Obvious proficiency can only be obtained through actual and continuous practice in the water itself. No amount of written or verbal instruction can enable on to swim on the first occasion he enters the water, but certain preliminary land exercises may be prescribed that will ensure his commencing on right lines.

Preliminary Land Practice

The Breaststroke: The best practice for learning to make the breaststroke correctly is not obtained by lying flat on the bed or music stool and acting the frog, but by indulging in certain scientific movements with each limb separately, the body occupying the upright or standing position. The boy should be lightly clad in singlet, trousers and belt and the following exercises may be gone through in the bedroom on rising or before retiring.

To Acquire the Correct Armstroke: Prepare for the breast stroke in the following manner – raise the hands in front of the chest with the thumbs and forefingers nearly touching, palms downward, fingers closes. The elbows should be close to the sides, the direction taken by the hands from the wrist to the finger tips slightly upwards. Then make cleanly the three following movements with a brief pause between each.

One: Lean the head well back and shoot the hands and arms out to their fullest extent upwards in the direction in which the hands are pointing. (Pause.)

Two: Separate the hands and bring them round at right-angles to the shoulder, turning the hands slightly outward at the same time, describing with each hand a quarter of a circle. (Pause.)

Three: Draw the elbows to the side and return the hands and forearms gracefully, not awkwardly to the position "prepare for breaststroke".

These three exercises should, on each occasion, be repeated at least a dozen times or until the pupil commences to feel fatigued, but they should not be hastened or performed in a slovenly manner.

Leg Movements: The correct movement of the legs in swimming is far more important and difficult than that of the arms, and the method now to be described must be most closely followed and persevered in. The speed without visible extra exertion that characterises nearly all good swimmers is due to the perfection of the leg movements, the action of the arms being quite of secondary consideration, this latter being, indeed, acquired almost instinctively. Each leg must of necessity be exercised separately, by three movements, which are as follows:

One: Place the hands on the hips, raise the right leg until its heel touches the knee of the left, the toes pointing downwards and the knee brought nearly at right angles to the body. (Pause.)

Two: Straighten the right leg and bring it to the ground one pace to the right of the centre of the body. (Pause.)

Three: Draw the right leg sharply to the left leg and drop the hands to "attention". Then the same drill should be gone through with the left leg, and then each exercised alternately for a dozen times, never accelerating the movements or getting careless in their performance.

Lastly, the following combined leg exercise should be taken, consisting also of three movements:

One: Place the hands on the hips, rise slowly on the ball of the foot, turn out and open the knees to their fullest extent, then sink slowly down until the backs of the thighs rest upon the calves of the legs. (Pause.)

Two: Spring up until the knees are straightened and immediately take a long pace to the right.*

Three: Draw the right foot smartly to the left and come to "attention".

The pupil will by this combined leg exercise instinctively learn that the propelling power comes from the downward stroke and the closing of the legs.

The boy who conscientiously practises the various movements just described will always be exercising and developing the right muscles and acquiring a correct style. He will be surprised at his rapid advancement over others who rely solely on haphazard practice in the water. He will have nothing to unlearn and will quickly outstrip any

---

*The pace should alternatively be taken to the left, and, when this is done, movement three will of course consist of bringing the left foot smartly to the right.

companion who enters the water at the same time as himself, but who is unpractised in the manner described. But at the same time it must again be emphasised that to be of value, the movements must be made slowly and carefully and never scurried through.

Having practised the foregoing exercises for a week or two the pupil will have gained sufficient knowledge to be of actual service to him, and should go to the water for practice, but the land exercises should not be abandoned, as they will always be of great value in maintaining a correct style, as well as constituting an exhilarating physical exercise that can be indulged in when the swimming bath is not available.

TAILOR BADGE

A Scout must cut out and sew, either by hand or machine, a Scout's shirt and shorts to fit himself.

Proceed to have measurement taken. The measures necessary are: 1. Length of inside leg-seam; 2. Length of side-seam; 3. Waist measurement; 4. Hip measurement; 5. Width at bottom.

A useful scale of measures is as follows:

SHORTS

		10 years	12 years	14 years	16 years
1.	Length of leg-seam	11"	11 1/2"	12"	13"
2.	Length of side-seam	20"	20 1/2"	21"	22"
3.	Waist measurement	27"	28"	33"	34"
4.	Hip measurement	31"	32"	33"	34"
5.	Width of bottoms	18"	19"	20"	21"

The diagram is cut to measurements for the 10 years size. Procure a sheet of brown paper, a tailor's crayon, an inchtape, square and a pair of scissors, and proceed to draft your shorts as follows:

The half of hip measurement is the scale that is $15\frac{1}{2}$" in this case. Draw a straight line, H to K = length of side seam, 20". Measure up 11" to A = length of leg seam. Mark S, $\frac{1}{4}$ scale. $3\frac{7}{8}$" up from A, which finds the hip line. Mark F $1\frac{1}{2}$" down from H, which finds the waist line. H to G = $\frac{1}{2}$ scale, that is $7\frac{3}{4}$". Go out from A to B $5\frac{1}{4}$", that is $\frac{1}{3}$ scale. Continue to C, ½ scale, 7¾. Continue to D, ⅔ scale = 10½". Join GC. E to F = ¼, waist measurement plus ½". Mark L ⅓ scale up from C. Draw curved line L to D. draw centre line BI at right angles to AB, IJ and IKA = ¼ of bottom measurement, that is 4½". Join DJ. This completes top sides. Cut the pattern out and lay it on the top of another piece of paper and draft the under sides.

Continue seat base line to M, 1/12 of scale from D = 1⅜". Draw DN through L. Curve at bottom to M. This gives you the seat seam. Mark O 1/2 out from J. Measure JKA = 9". Place tape at 9" on O and measure to P. 18" plus 1" for seams = 19"

Measure T to S = 7¾". Place tape at 7¾" on L and measure to V, 15½" plus 1" for seams and 1" for ease = 17½". Measure EF = 7¼". Place tape at 7¼" on Q and measure to R. 13½" plus 1" for seams = 14½". Draw side line, RVP. This completes the under sides.

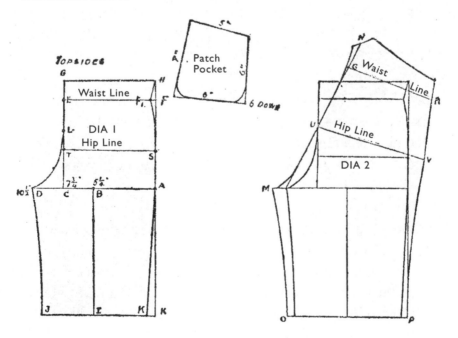

Cut this pattern out also. Take the top side pattern, lay it on the double cloth and chalk out. Proceed in like manner with the under sides, taking care that plenty of cloth is left for fly and patch pocket, and pocket facings. Leave 2" upturn at bottom and leave an outlet of at least 1" on seat seam when cutting out.

It would avoid misunderstanding if a practical tailor was consulted regarding the making up of these shorts, as it is most difficult to explain without a practical demonstration.

SHIRTS

For simplicity, it is well to fix a scale of sizes, viz:

	10 years.	12 years.	14 years.	16 years.
	Size 3.	Size 4.	Size 5.	Size 6.
Body,	29"x 30"	30"x 22"	32"x 24"	34"x 25"
Sleeves	14"x8"x 5"	15"x 8$\frac{1}{4}$"x 5"	15$\frac{1}{2}$"x 8$\frac{1}{2}$"x 5$\frac{1}{4}$"	16"x8$\frac{3}{4}$"x5$\frac{1}{2}$"
Wrist	8$\frac{1}{2}$"x4"	8$\frac{1}{2}$"x4"	9"x4$\frac{1}{2}$"	9$\frac{1}{2}$"x5"
Yoke	18"x4"x2$\frac{1}{2}$"	20"x4$\frac{1}{2}$"x2"	22"x4$\frac{1}{2}$"x3"	23"x4$\frac{1}{2}$"x 3"
Breast pleat	11"x3$\frac{1}{2}$"	12"x3$\frac{1}{2}$"	12$\frac{1}{2}$" x 3$\frac{1}{2}$"	13" x 3$\frac{1}{2}$"
Neck	13"	13$\frac{1}{2}$"	14"	14$\frac{1}{2}$"

Shirt This diagram is drawn for size 3 to $\frac{1}{8}$, scale. Take 58" material, that is twice the length of shirt, and fold as in diagram, leaving top side 2" longer than under side. Mark A and B 1$\frac{1}{2}$" from edge C and D 8" from top. Curve out scye as shown.

Sleeve Draw BR 1$\frac{1}{2}$" more than length of sleeve given, that is 15$\frac{1}{2}$" square, from B to T 8" and from R to S 5". Join TS, mark D 1$\frac{1}{2}$" from T. curve from D to B to fit armhole in shirt. Notice that this is only the half of sleeve. When cutting keep BR to double edge of cloth.

Yoke E to F = EB + ¼" for centre seam, EG squared 4" down FH = 2". Join GH. This also is only half yoke.

Wrist band – IJ = 8½". IJ and M = 4". IL and JK = 3".

Breast Pleat = 11½" x 3½".

Patch Pocket – NO = 4½" + 2" for box pleat. NP = 5". Blunt corners at bottom. Flap to button, 1½" deep.

Shoulder Straps – 6" x 1½" at neck and 1" at point, to button.

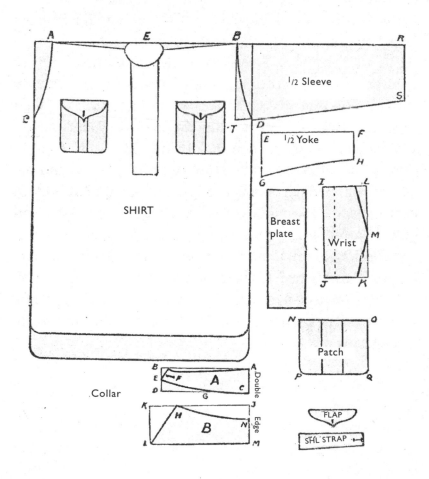

Collar Consists of two parts – A, the band and B, the turn over. It is also drawn in half.

A – AB = 1½" more than size of collar required, 6½" + 1" = 7¾". D and C 2" down. Mark E 1" down from B, and G 3" from C. join GE as marked, and at F hollow ½". Join BA as marked.

B – Make JK 1" more than AB, that is 8¾". L and M 3" down. Join LM. Mark down from J 1½" to N, back from K to 2½" to H. join HL and HN with a curve as marked. This completes top which is joined to A, the band at BA and HN.

The wristbands, yokes, patch pocket etc., are found from the balance of cloth cut from width of shirt.

It is advisable for a Boy Scout to get his mother or sister to instruct him in the making of his shirt. A practical demonstration being worth books of theory. The main features in method of proceeding are to start by stitching on yoke right across shirt. Then cut down front of shirt from E, 9" for breast pleat. The side-seams are now stitched and the bottom hemmed. Note, to leave vents of about 7" at bottom of sides, finished strongly with a gusset. Sleeves are made and fitted to armholes, keeping seam of sleeve to side-seam of shirt. Neck is now hollowed out to exact size – a difficult item, requiring experience. Collar is made and sewed on. Finish by fixing patch pockets and shoulder straps. Care must be taken to make nice, tidy button-holes and that the buttons are sewed firmly on.

TELEGRAPHIST BADGE

A Scout must understand simple electric circuits; be able to send out and receive by Morse Key and Sounder, a message at the rate of 30 letters a minute; be able to explain construction of, and do simple repairs to, single needle telegraph instruments and understand the elementary principles of a wireless telegraphy installation.

MORSE'S TELEGRAPH KEY

WOODMAN BADGE

A Scout must fell a tree with a felling axe, properly; know how to use a saw for felling big trees; know the different species of trees by their appearance, and their respective uses as timber; know a well-grown tree (i.e., one useful for timber purposes) from a bad one; know the trade names and dimensions of planks, scantlings – and how to measure timber; know the general principles of levering, hauling, stacking timber and bark usual in the locality; sharpen an axe on grindstone, and know how to use wedges.

Timber is the term applied to all trees, whether growing or felled, which yield wood suitable for constructional purposes; that is to say, wood that can be converted into beams, rafters, boards etc.

Timber may be roughly divided into two classes of wood- hard and soft. The chief difference in appearance between the trees is that hardwood trees have broad leaves of various sizes, such as oak, beech, ash, walnut, plane, elm birch; on the other hand, softwood trees have leaves like needles or bristles, the pine, spruce and fir trees belonging to this class.

The British Oak, which is found in all temperate parts of Europe, is the most lasting of all native woods. Apart from it's use as timber, the bark is valuable on account of the tannin it contains, which is used for tanning purposes.

The acorns are excellent food for swine.

The wood from the oak combines strength and durability

with hardness and elasticity. Before the introduction of iron for ship-building, oak was largely used in the construction of hulls of ships. It is now used in architectural work, cabinet-making, carving, millwork, coopering etc.

The Beech almost equals the oak in size. The bark is smooth and of a grey colour, and is covered with hard, wooden knobs, which are abortive buds. It thrives best on light soils, and its roots are not very deep. Grass does not grow very readily under a beech tree.

The wood is hard and solid but brittle, and is very liable to rot and become worm eaten if exposed to the air. It is, therefore, not used for house carpentry. However, if kept under water, it is very durable, and, for this reason, is largely used for weirs, sluices etc. It is also used for making chairs, tables, and many small wooden articles in daily use.

The raspings of the wood are used in the preparation of vinegar. The wood also makes excellent charcoal, the ashes yielding a lot of potash. The bark is sometimes used for tanning when oak bark is not available.

Fir Trees: Fir is the name often given erroneously to all pine and fir trees, but in the proper sense it applies only to the silver fir and spruce tree. These trees are distinguished from the pines and larches by having their needlelike leaves singly on the shoots and not in clusters or tufts. The cones are composed of thin, rounded, closely packed scales.

The Norway Spruce is a lofty tree with a straight, tapering trunk. The long, cylindrical cones grow principally at the end of the upper branches. These cones are purple at first, but become green later, and eventually light brown. The tree is in the best condition for felling between seventy and ninety years old.

The wood is white and sometimes very knotty. It is known as white deal, white Norway, and Danzig deal. It is used for flooring, joists and rafters. If not exposed to the weather, it is almost as durable as pine, but, as it is not so resinous, it is not so well adapted for outdoor uses. The younger and smaller trees are very durable, especially when the bark is allowed to remain on them, and in this state they are used for scaffolding poles etc.

Pine: The Scottish pine (sometimes erroneously called the Scotch fir) has spikey leaves, in pairs about 1½ inches long, with cones about the same length. As the tree grows, the lower branches drop off, so that the pine tree has usually a very long trunk with foliage only at the top. The timber is very valuable, being resinous and durable. It is known as red deal, or red pine, and is used in house and ship carpentry. Tar, pitch, resin, lamp-black and common turpentine are products of the pine tree.

Larch: The common larch is a stately tree, with tall, erect trunk, gradually tapering from root to top. The larch is distinguishable from the pine and fir by its leaves. The spikes or leaves are scattered singly on the young shoots of the season, but thy grow in small tufts or bunches on the older branchlets, each tuft surrounding what appears to be a small abortive shoot. The cones are about an inch in length.

The wood is close and compact, and in colour varies from a brownish yellow to a deep reddish colour. It is very tough, and, if properly seasoned, will not shrink or split. It is, however, liable to warp or bend if not properly seasoned. It is often left floating in water for a year after felling. Its strength and toughness make it valuable for dockyard and naval purposes. It is also used for fences and by wheelwrights.

The Birch is a very hardy tree. It has round, slender branches, and serrated, deciduous leaves. The bark is in fine, soft layers, the outer part which peels off in thin, white, papery sheets.

The wood is tough and tenacious, and is used largely by carriage-builders, upholsters, and turners. The flexible branches are used for brooms. The bark is very durable and impermeable to water. On this account, it is used largely in Russia for roofing and for making boxes and jars, and also for making a kind of shoe. The birch also yields an oil which is used in making Russian leather. The pleasant odour of Russian leather is due to this oil.

The Elm: The wood of the elm is valued for its great strength, toughness and closeness of texture. It is the least liable to split of any timber, and does not become rotten in water. It is, therefore, used for keels of boats, spokes of wheels, foundation piles, and wet planking.

The large knots with which the tree is covered are much used in decorative cabinetwork, on account of their beautiful appearance when cut and polished. The bark is used in dyeing and sugar-refining.

The Common Ash is a beautiful ornamental tree, but is very injurious to crops or grass in its immediate neighbourhood. The leaves are deciduous, and are what is called pinnated, with a terminal leaflet. It generally has a smooth stem, and rises to a height of 100 to 150 feet.

The wood ranks next to oak for strength and durability, and is adapted to a great number of uses. It is white, tough and hard, and is used by wheelwrights, cartwrights, coachbuilders, turners and jointers. The young trees are as valuable for timber as the old, and the wood is tougher when the growth has been rapid. The ash grows in almost any soil, but prefers a loamy one, and it will grow in exposed and elevated situations where other trees will not.

The Common Holly is a well-known ornament of parks and shrubberies. Its leaves are evergreen, leathery, shining and spinous. The fruit is a small scarlet berry, and affords food for birds in winter, but to man its effects are purgative and emetic, and, in large quantities, poisonous. Bird-lime is sometimes made from the inner bark.

The wood is almost as white as ivory, and is used by musical instrument makers, cabinetmakers and turners, and also for wood-engraving. Handles for tools and handles for metal teapots are also made from it. The name holly is supposed to be derived from its being used for decorating churches at Christmas time, on account of which it was therefore called the "Holly" tree.

Hawthorn is a shrub or small tree, which is much planted in hedges or for ornament. Its height varies from six or eight to twenty-five feet. The leaves are deciduous, roundish, and three to five lobbed. The hawthorn is most valuable as a hedge plant. The young hedges are called quicks, or quick-sets, because they are used to make quick (meaning living) fences. The wood is used for handles of tools etc.

Poplars: There are many varieties of poplars. It is a large tree, of rapid growth. The leaves, which are deciduous, are broad, heart or lozenge-shaped. It is not of much use as timber, as the wood is generally white, soft and light. It is sometimes used for scaffold poles. The wood of the grey poplar is harder and better, and is used for flooring, barrows etc. it does not catch fire so readily as some woods, so is preferable to pine deal in the neighbourhood of fireplaces.

Willow: The willow is of the same class of tree as the poplar. Some are very small plants, especially when grown in the arctic or alpine regions. There are tiny ones in the mountains of Scotland which only grow to about an inch from the ground. Some of the species, however, grow to a large size, and are of remarkably rapid growth. The wood of some willows is very tough and durable, tough light and soft. In olden times, it was used for shields. Nowadays, cricket bats are made from willow, also paddles of steamboats

Chestnut: This tree, which must not be confused with the horse chestnut, is closely allied to the beech. It is grown largely as a fruit tree. The nuts are used as food, either roasted or boiled; they are also sometimes ground down into flour and made into a bread. When planted as a fruit tree it is generally grafted.

The timber is durable and hard, and is used among many other things for house-building and furniture-making. The bark is used for tanning, but is only worth about half the price of oak bark. Young chestnut trees are used for hop-poles.

The Horse Chestnut is a wholly distinct tree from the chestnut. Its rapid growth, stately appearance and exceptionally fine foliage and blossom, make it greatly liked for parks and gardens. The timber, however, is soft, and of very little value.

THE
BOY SCOUT'S
STAND BY.

WITH SECCOTINE he can make or mend a thousand things. As Bookbinder, Carpenter, Camper, Electrician, Handyman, Leather Worker, Photographer, he needs SECCOTINE all the time. Every day he will find new uses for it, every day he will like his useful friend better and better.

He will have no trouble whatever in preparing his material, SECCOTINE is always ready without heating. There are no troublesome corks of bottles to get out, for SECCOTINE is put up in tubes of varying sizes, each of them carrying with it a spike or pin. With this the cone at the top is pierced, and after use the spike or pin is replaced in the cone, where it acts as a stopper. As the main part of this stopper is always in the soft material there is never any difficulty in withdrawing it. Care should be taken to press out what is wanted while holding the fold at the *bottom* of the tube—the cone helps in applying the material where it may be wanted. When it is applied, the only care needed is to see that the joint gets a proper time for drying (in ordinary temperature).

If broken vessels of glass, china, or delf are to be mended so as to hold hot or cold liquids, then FIRMAS (Heat Seccotine) should be used. But repairs with FIRMAS require stoving in an ordinary kitchen oven.

Seccotine tubes are sold in the British Islands at 4½d. (vest pocket size with tin box), 6d. and 9d. (in cartons.)

The word "SECCOTINE" is a registered trade mark.

On Sale in Shops everywhere.

McCAW, STEVENSON & ORR, Limited,
The Linenhall Works, BELFAST.

SCOUTCRAFT.

"You know what 'Scouting for Boys' says about boots, and you turn up in those. Call yourself a scout—look at them . . . ."

"They're clean, aren't they?"

"Oh, they're clean, but are they waterproof?"

"You're looking at the uppers, they're going before the soles. I could stand in a puddle for a week and not get wet feet. They're "DRI-PED" soled and "Dri-ped's" absolutely waterproof?"

"But the uppers look worn out."

"DRI-PED" soles often outlast the uppers. I've worn these boots for twelve months, day after day, without having them re-soled, and they're still good, and waterproof, and as comfortable as old boots."

"Well, you know what 'Scouting for Boys' says . . ."

"And you know how many badges I've got so . . . ."

(It must be confessed that there are times when scouts are sometimes not quite polite to one another.)

HAVE YOUR
SHOES SOLED WITH
Dri-ped

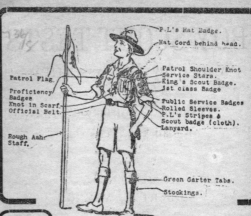